[handwritten:] P J Howl   1969-74
Colin Fraser. 1967-1972.
Bob Sawer   '84 !!

[barcode:] CH00829794

A Life,
One up on the
Ocean Wave

by
Charles Saxby

[handwritten:] To [scribbled out] and [scribbled out]
Christmas   2007.
C Saxby

Published by Brent Publications

The material in this book is copyright
and may not be reproduced in any form whatsoever
without the specific permission of the author

ISBN No. 978 0 948706 25 7

Printed by Basildon Printing Company Limited
Fleet House, Armstrong Road, South Benfleet, Essex SS7 4FH

Foreword

When we look at people we only see their physical being. What we cannot see are the things that are locked up in their minds consisting of amassed memories and personal experiences gathered over many years. So it was that some years after my father died I came to realise that I had missed the opportunity to find out more about his and my mother's life together; Mum having passed away at the grand old age of 94, some years after Dad who left us at the age of 84. They made them tough in those days!

What I did know about Dad was that as a young man he was employed as a gramophone engineer at a company in the Whitechapel Road. He consequently joined the army at the outbreak of World War I serving with the Devonshire Regiment. He was unfortunate to lose the use of one lung during the conflicts in the trenches in France. This was due to the lack of proper equipment needed to defend themselves against the mustard gas attacks perpetrated by the German enemy. In fact the only protection they had was a wet piece of cloth which they held over their nose and mouth. If no water was to be had they would pee on the cloth and use that! It was early days and the equipment was in short supply. Unfortunately this did not work well and Dad inhaled gas which destroyed one of his lungs leaving him with a lifelong problem. He also received a number of shrapnel wounds with the small bits being lost in his body and these in fact stayed with him until the day he died.

After his service in France he was transferred to Mesopotamia (Iraq) where his duties were to help guard the railways that were being built there by the British Government. On his demobilisation from the army he returned to England only to find that the country was in the grip of unemployment caused by the conflict it had been through. He attended a government-sponsored course in shoe mending to enable him to return to working life. That was not too successful as full-time employment because there were so many of the returning soldiers doing the same course, but it did give him the skill to make sure that we children had well repaired footwear! He finally settled in a job as a maintenance man in a factory making metal mesh guards for both machinery and underwater cables. It did not pay too well but we managed as a family and he always made sure we had a reasonable lifestyle.

After the realisation of the opportunities I had missed in the past I decided to put my own story on paper for the benefit of my offspring or indeed anyone who would find it readable.

A Life, One up on the Ocean Wave

Early Years

I was born on the 3rd July 1931 in the London Hospital Whitechapel which is within the sound of Bow bells and means that I qualify for the title of Cockney. This being the term used to describe a true Londoner. While being honoured to be one of the same I am not very fond of the way they converse even though it stretches way back into history.

My earliest memories are getting a bit hazy now due to my 76 years. I do recall the more memorable ones due to their outstanding influence at the time. The Saxby family lived upstairs in three rooms of a terraced house at 30 Royston Street, Bethnal Green. There was my Mum Alice, Dad Charles, my sisters Alice and Gladys and of course myself. The house was typical of the period; no electricity and only gas for cooking and lighting, with an iron range that contained the coal fire for heating and some cooking. There were no taps upstairs as the water pressure was very low and all water had to be collected from the yard tap and carried up in large white enamel jugs. The only toilet available was situated in the backyard and nicknamed the 'thunder box' and was shared by both families. After dark the only lighting available in the 'thunder box' was by means of a candle in a holder fixed to the wall. When this was lit it made eerie shadows on the walls and ceilings that would cause a small boy to have frightening thoughts. So as often as not one of my family would have to keep me company and wait outside while I completed my visit!

Living standards in those days would be quite unacceptable in the present time, with the absence of bathrooms, except in the houses of well-off families. One had to do with sponge downs in the privacy of the bedroom, usually on Sunday when Mum would make sure you had clean underclothes to put on afterwards. There was a galvanized bathtub that would be taken into the kitchen and filled with hot water from numerous kettles and saucepans that were heated on the kitchen range. Because it was such an effort to do this the bath water was shared, you just hoped that you would not be the last one in!

The last and more favourable method of keeping clean was to visit the York Hall Slipper Baths. It was a less complicated and more enjoyable method. After purchasing your ticket and receiving a large white towel and a small bar of soap you would take your place in the waiting room often filled with grumpy old men. The wait always took a long time, but as I usually went with three or four lads we cut down the boredom by skylarking about much to the annoyance of the grumpy old men. When it was your turn to go in, the attendant would call your ticket number and fill the bath up to the regulation height of six inches of water. The bath was so big the amount of hot water was quite adequate for a small boy to swim in. I spent the maximum amount of time in there and would come out looking like a pink shrivelled plum.

Another nasty thing about that era were the bugs! These were the so-called bed bugs. Owing to the lack of insecticide in those days and the practice of putting wallpaper up with flour and water, the conditions were perfect for these horrible little creatures to breed. They would be attracted by the warmth of the human body and while lying asleep in bed would extract blood though your skin, this would leave some unsightly marks when you awoke. The difficulty in keeping them under control was a problem; either shooing them out of their hiding place and squashing them, that method was quite messy, or coating the worst areas with paraffin, that was very smelly and used to make us all feel quite sick. One would never be allowed to squash a bug on the wallpaper as that would leave a nasty mark, thus spoiling the look of the place. It was hard for my mother to keep the home clean, as there were no vacuum cleaners, no detergents, in fact only the basic equipment like a bucket of water and scrubbing brush. But I know she managed well enough.

After all these tales of woe, one would be led to believe that you could not possibly have any nostalgic feelings for times like these, but strangely I have. The memories of a friendly kitchen warmed by the coal fire in the cast iron range, on top of which sat the kettle that was always on the boil and singing softly. Am I waxing lyrical, or are they just fond childhood memories. The kitchen range was the focal point that my mother took great pride in. It was always blackleaded until it shone and the hearth whitened. And God help anyone who made a mess there!

Play time in those days was fun, not only for the children but for adults too. As there was no television or other visual distractions, the parents would sit on the doorstep, or at the open windows to watch the youngsters playing cricket or rounders and give them verbal support. Young people, could in those days spend all day, as we often used to, at Victoria Park, with supplies of mixed up lemonade and bags of broken biscuits. We enjoyed the wonderful facilities of the boating lake, swings, paddling pool, and most of all our own little bit of countryside without the fear of molestation which we see all too often these days.

Most crimes then were seemingly under control due to the harsh penalties that they incurred. A

2

fact that is sadly not the case at the present time. It was a known fact, that you could leave the street door key on a piece of string through the letterbox so that all the family could have access without the danger of being burgled! I am of the opinion that we were all in the same boat and that nobody had anything worth stealing. I am also of the opinion that crimes in this present age will reach such large proportions that the authorities will be forced to return the death penalty for wilful murder, and appropriate penalties for associated crimes.

Leaving these sad thoughts behind, I would rather remember more pleasant days like Sunday mornings, when my Dad would go down to the local newspaper shop for his 'News of the World' and at the same time buy me either the 'Film Fun' or the 'Playbox' comics. Armed with these I would settle back in bed, with a cup of tea Mum had brought to me. I would retreat into my own little world, happy days.

My Dad was of the Victorian age when father was boss. If there was any naughtiness he would reach for his thick leather belt. Not that he would use it very often but it made you realise that you had to do as you were told. We never had any real holidays as such; but Dad always made sure that whenever possible we spent days on the beach at Southend where we would paddle, have lovely ice cream and on one occasion we had a family photo taken in an open top sports car belonging to the photographer. Dad did his very best for us, but times were hard for him, made so by the lack of employment.

During the First World War he had served as a sapper in the Devonshire Regiment and fought in all the big battles in France and in consequence suffered the agonies of warfare, they had no masks and suffered gas attacks which caused him losing a lung. Tight puttees caused him to have varicose veins that plagued him for years after.

Before the First World War Dad was employed as a gramophone mechanic. The type you wind up with the sound trumpet on the top. But on returning from serving his country all that was gone. What was left was life on the dole. The depression that followed was soul destroying, but we obviously came through it and Dad finished up working as a maintenance man in a factory producing heavy wire mesh. This place was to play a large part in my early life.

Dad had two brothers, William and Arthur. Uncle Will was an amateur magician. While Uncle Arthur emigrated to begin a new life in Australia, and after having three sons started a regular tribe of Saxby's down under.

3

So it was we lived our lives under the best conditions we could. They say that when you're at the bottom the only way is up and so it was. Our position did change, but in a strange way.

The year was now 1939 and I was eight, we had lived our lives as described up to this point, it was then that the Second World War was declared, and once again everybody's existence was turned upside down. Dad by this time was too old to be called up again, thank goodness. I can remember fairly clearly the day war was declared. I remember at the time I was playing with a toy train on the fireside fender as the announcement was made. Even at that age I realised the seriousness of the occasion. Not long after that, the air raid warning sounded as a practice, everyone went to pieces not knowing what to do. I sat with my sisters on the front door step until the 'all clear' sounded and we could all breathe again. I am not sure about the time factor, but it was decided that my sister Gladys and I were to be evacuated to a safer place. After much organising with the school, lots of packing and lots of tears both of us were off to Kings Lynn, in Norfolk, situated on the River Wash. I would be lying if I said it was not exciting. I had never been away as far as that, especially without my Mum and Dad.

We arrived in a confused state, and had to wait around for a very long time before someone came over to us and as you might say adopt us. We were lucky in as much that it was a young couple who put themselves out for us. I remember the first thing they gave us to eat was a packet of Smarties. (No rationing as yet) The first few weeks were quite confusing, I learned how to go scrumping; and how to get stuck in the mud on the banks of the River Wash but I don't remember ever going to school. I'm sure that I wasn't there long enough. We missed home a lot and pined for the family, so it was decided that we return to London.

Of course the idea of evacuation was to keep the children out of harm's way but children are very susceptible to change and cannot rationally cope with it. So it was that we returned home, but to our surprise, we had moved! During our absence the family had decided to share a house with my Granny and my mother's sister Aunt Lizzie. This address was 24 Gawber Street. A house which has a long association with our family even to this very day. The property had always been occupied by my mother's family. Once again we were living two families to a house but with a difference, we were all related! We soon settled down to a good relationship.

Granny liked to have stewed eels for her Saturday tea followed by a jug of milk stout! Nectar of the gods she called it. She had an ancient parrot in a large cage. This bird at times escaped and attacked any strangers in the room usually by settling on the poor soul's head and sinking its claws and pecking the scalp. I was reliably informed by Aunt Lizzie that the old bird turned savage after being tormented by my Dad and his brother Uncle Will. Apparently when Dad was courting my Mum he and Will would turn up at Gawber Street and make themselves comfortable one either side of the parrot cage, light their pipes and puffing smoke across to one another leaving the poor old polly a screeching wreck!

My recollections of Granny Martin (Mum's maiden name) are a little bit hazy but I do remember her always seeming to be dressed in black. The Saturday jobs I had to do to get any pocket money were as I have said to get Granny's eels, and a jug of milk stout from the Bottle and Jug bar in the 'Florist' pub in Globe Road. It's probably a trendy art gallery now. My other job was to polish the brass stair rods that held the tatty carpet in place. We had our pride you see.

I remember the appearance of a man with his barrel organ, who by turning the handle was able to play the good old favorites like 'Roll out the Barrel' etc. He always seemed to position himself half way down the street to get maximum effect, with cap in hand for the donations he was hoping to get, turning the handle of the organ for all he was worth, for about thirty minutes. Having done his stint in our vicinity he would move on to the next street. There were two other buskers that visited on Saturday, one was a very tall man in a long coat who played a penny whistle extremely loudly. He was partially sighted. I always felt sorry for him and usually found a coin or two to put in the tin cup he had tied to his coat belt. The other busker had a horse and cart, the cart was fitted with a small merry-go-round that could be operated by him, once again turning a handle. For a donation of say, a couple of empty jam jars - early recycling, a child could have a ride on the merry-go-round. That is what his business was, rags, bottles and bones. I don't know what happened to all the items after he collected them, but it was a fun way of getting rid of your rubbish, for the children that is.

Granny Martin was eventually taken poorly, and had to go into a nursing home, where she finally passed away. She was brought home to Gawber Street, and laid to rest in her coffin on four chairs in the front room; this being the special room that was always kept clean and polished for special occasions. The neighbours would then be allowed at their leisure to come in to pay their last respects. This was the norm in those days, a more reverential family way.

I have no doubt that the same was done for Grandad Martin, but then I did not know him as he had passed on before I was around. I also did not know my grandparents on my father's side, but was very proud to know that Grandad worked as a brewer for forty years in Truman's Brewery in Brick

Lane. This was a fact borne out to me when later on in life I was employed at Truman's for a short while doing some engineering work, and was able to see Grandad's name on the Scroll of Honour, one of the first entrants. This scroll was situated in the main reception area and can you believe it, apparently he didn't drink!

We were into the first year of the war, and after the raids and the dogfights going on with the English and German aeroplanes, it was decided that I should once again be evacuated. So it was that myself and eldest sister Alice, who was married to a sailor named Charles Horton, and her baby Carol left London. The three of us were shipped off to a place called Nordon just outside Rochdale in Lancashire.

Unfortunately, on arrival Alice and myself were split up into two different houses. I went to live with a family in a way that was completely alien to me. The main meals seemed to consist of baked beans and chips, I cannot ever remember having meat there. Maybe I did but I do not remember. There was no bath, and the bedroom I shared with their son had a pot under the bed that was stained brown and filled the room with a ghastly smell. The good thing about my staying there was that they owned a smallholding with goats, sheep and geese. Not having been in contact with anything like this before I was in my element. I even had my own rabbit in a cage for the very first time. One of my daily jobs was to feed the animals before I went to school - wonderful! I think that an enthusiastic volunteer was just what they wanted but I didn't mind, I was in heaven. I cannot be sure how long I was there, but it was long enough for me to start school, and to establish myself in a paper round.

I suppose I must have been at Nordon for about four to five months. The school seemed to be a school for lunatics, whose main aim seemed to be making life as difficult as possible for us evacuees. For example; one little lunatic game they liked to play was the electrocution chicken test. This was done by having about ten kids holding the next one's hand, the last one placing his hand on something solid for a good earth, then the first kid in the line would stick his fingers in a live light socket! The result would be that the electricity travelled harmlessly until it reached the last kid in the line who was contacting earth and that's when you heard the loud pitched scream of pain. You can bet your bottom dollar it would be an evacuee that was taking the chicken test. Hardly the playtime game in the same league as skipping and football was it?

It was during this time that I decided to try my hand at doing a paper round after being shown the houses to which I had to make deliveries. My job was to be at the shop by 6.30am ready to load up with a heavy bag of newspapers that I had to trundle around the almost pitch black streets. You can imagine the terror I sometimes felt in the dark, with the wind lashing the bushes and trees. And the long walk up the garden paths to reach the gloomy doorways and behind every bush there seemed to lurk a monster. Well it seemed like that to a little boy anyway.

My time in Nordon came to an end when my concerned Mum, after a visit, decided it was time for me to return home. My sister Alice stayed because she lived with a very nice family and of course she had a young baby, Carol, to think about.

I arrived back to find London in the grip of the blitz. To my amazement I found that during my absence, a metal cage with a thick iron top had been fitted in the front room, this being my future bed. The idea being that your chances would be better when the house came down if bombed. It was a nightly event to remove the wire mesh front, crawl inside and into my bed while the front was put back on and hoping to God that it wasn't my turn to get blown up that night or any other night come to that.

Yes, the early innocent days are now past, and we had been projected into a world gone mad, for the blitz had by now reached a point that was really frightening.

The one oasis for our family was the fact that my Dad's employers had the foresight before the war started to have deep shelters installed under their premises. These shelters were completely fitted out with bunk beds, toilets and cooking facilities. The company offered the use of the shelters to its employees families after the day's production was done. Our family took up the offer.

So at about six o'clock every evening we packed up our necessary goods and moved into the shelter, about one and a half miles away. We would stay there all night in comparative safety. It would be silly to say complete safety for nowhere in that area was at all safe.

During our nights there, the muffled roar of the anti-aircraft guns, the crash of falling bombs was almost too much to bear. On vacating the shelter in the morning, the full effect of the night could be seen as we picked our way past burning buildings.

This went on night after night and one particular morning as we made our way home, we were amazed to see hundreds of bodies being laid out on the pavement outside Bethnal Green underground station. This we found out later was the result of panic that took place the previous evening when people waiting to use the underground as a shelter were frightened by rockets being fired at enemy aircraft; this resulted in people falling down the stairs. I believe that one hundred and seventy souls died because the people behind pushing forward were unaware of what was happening at the front and were tumbling

7

on top of the fallen bodies and as a result crushing and suffocating those on the ground. A memorial exists to mark this terrible disaster in the form of a plaque on the wall in the entrance to the station.

During the periods when there were no actual air raids taking place, we were allowed to emerge from the shelter to stretch our legs and at least ease the tension by seeing something different other than the concrete walls of the shelter. So during my wanderings around this now quiet factory, which incidentally was the place that I was destined a few years later to start my working life, my interest was aroused by the large round cast iron coal fire heater they kept going all night. The fire was warm, friendly and glowing surrounded by the darkness of the factory workshop. The top of the cast iron fire would be glowing red hot and you could spit on the red hot plate and watch the little spurts of steam spiral upwards. There was one unpleasant thing about the nights, and that was rats! To combat these, rat cages baited with bits of food were placed at all the rat runs. My friendly image of the old fire was shattered when one night as I was standing there warming myself one of the night watchmen came along with a rat trapped in a cage, opened the door of the fire and dropped the cage into it! I was slightly shocked at the cruelty. And when the cage was lifted out after about ten minutes there was of course no trace of the rat. But the cruelty was no more than the terrible things that were happening to people all around us at that very moment.

During 1940 saw the event of a new addition to our family. No! not a baby, this time it was a fully grown person. This came about when a friend of my sister Gladys, named Edna Hardy, was placed in a difficult position by her mother deserting the family. The situation became worse when her father got his call-up papers for the army. Her younger brother found a place to live with his aunt and it was agreed that Edna would temporarily stay with us. Tragically, her father was later killed in action. So it turned out that she became our unofficially adopted sister and with us she remained into her adulthood and indeed until she was happily married.

The end of the second year of war had been fantastically lucky for us, metaphorically speaking of course, for we had bombs falling all around our house but none near enough to do any real damage. Only the odd incendiary bombs through the roofs of nearby houses in the street, and these were quickly put out with a great deal of help from my Dad. Just five hundred yards down the street and through Sugar Loaf Walk, was the little park in which was situated an anti-aircraft battery, and the accompanying searchlights. I was surprised that our area didn't come in for more attention from the enemy bombers.

My sister Gladys used to cross the park on her way to work every day and I presume that, as she did, a particular soldier, Robert Heudibourke, used to chat her up. Well it worked, for some time later they were married. It was a strange name, and I know she was a bit worried about taking it on. I think it was a European name. Gladys eventually joined the Land Army. This organisation was formed for girls to work on the farms, as most of the young men had been conscripted to the armed forces which left the farmers very short of labour. Food was of the highest necessity in this besieged country.

Working only from memory I will attempt to describe the Land Army's uniform, and how proud we all were to see Gladys come home in it. The hat was broad brimmed a bit like the Australian bush hat and beige in colour. A khaki shirt and tie and this was topped off with a green heavy jumper with leather scuff pads and Land Army insignias at the shoulders. Next the trousers; these were in the form of corduroy jodhpurs also in a beige colour, and finally, heavy khaki socks with brown boots. An outfit that fell in with the countryside perfectly. I explain the uniform because unfortunately she never had a photograph of herself dressed for the farm.

She and Bob married in 1943 and went on to have three girls, Barbara, Joan and Anne. I am afraid that Gladys and Bob have passed away, so sadly we have only our memories of them. Also I have not seen the girls for a very long time, ah well!

Into the third year of the war and we had seen the worst of the bombing. The Blitzkrieg, as Herr Hitler had called it, had not smashed us into submission, but what it did do was to weld the whole nation into a defiant and angry people with one aim in mind, to destroy the Nazis!

As the bombing had eased a good deal it was decided that we would no longer go on the long journey up to Dad's company's excellent shelters. We would put our faith in the newly built bomb shelter that was opposite our house. The shelter was solidly built of brick and concrete, and could stand a good deal of punishment. The only drawback was that it was just below a seven storey block of flats. If they were brought down by the bombing the shelter would really have been in trouble. So the routine would be to go to bed at home until the air raid warning sounded, then with all your belongings run across to the shelter. This could happen as much as three times a night.

The shelter did not have any lighting, so candles had to be taken. There were metal bunks fitted to accommodate one for a long stay, so a certain amount of bedding also had to be taken. Sometimes a board game was taken, to be played in the flickering candle light, until a bomb fell within the vicinity, and the blast of air that followed blew the candles out!

After all these restless nights the exhaustion that followed became a big problem for both young and old. We struggled on through 1942 with all the different military theatres of war happening in the world all with stories different from mine. And so we moved into 1943.

This year was to be quite full of memories for me, I had left junior school at Globe Road Primary and started at Cranbrook. Going from a lovely warm and friendly place, with nice teachers and familiar surroundings, to the more competitive and more aggressive school friends was quite a shock. But I soon adapted, and later on I was very sad to lose a lot of my new chums due to the bombing and new weapons that were eventually used.

One blight of my schooldays was the fact that I had to wear short trousers. I was longing to have long trousers and have some street-cred! Dad said that I would be able to have them when I was thirteen. Mum always made my short trousers out of suitable materials that she was able to obtain, this was because of the difficulty of clothing coupons and availability. Everything was rationed. Mum was very good at making the trousers but unable to make the fly hole, and substituted with a little slit in the front, just enough to get my willie out, and small enough not to be noticed! On one occasion during a fitting session of a new pair, my sister Alice on instruction from Mum was pulling them off me for some more adjustments, and not realising that one of the long cottons used in the making had wrapped its self around my willie, so the harder she pulled to get them off the more I yelled until at last everyone realised what was happening!

The year had its numerous incidents when on our way home from school, our route took us along Green Street with all the shops that had candy striped screens hanging down on each side. We all loved to give these screens a good punch as we passed. This particular day the butcher had moved his butchers block behind his screen. I came along, gave it a whopping punch that resulted in my wrist very nearly being broken! Other incidents that happened were brick throwing fights with rival gangs. That resulted on two occasions in me having my head split open wide enough to have stitches put in at the hospital. These fights usually took place on the bombed-out building sites, where the ammunition was plentiful, but so was the dirt and dust.

I contracted a very nasty condition called Scabies. This is usually caused by malnutrition and germs lurking in places such as bombed-out sites. The germs are self explanatory, the malnutrition was probably caused by the severe rationing at that time. Scabies causes large open sores to appear, mainly in the leg area. The treatment at the Lefevre Road Clinic was to be immersed in warm sulphur baths three times a week. A ghastly experience that I would not wish on my worst enemy. Not only was the smell overpowering, but the indignity suffered under the ministrations of the nursing staff, who had a lot of patience. But they cured me in the end, and I was very grateful for that.

The war moved on into 1943, and then we had the worst winter in decades, just to make things even more difficult for us all. The bad weather persisted for a long time allowing the permafrost to get a good hold everywhere. As most of the goods were transported by horse and cart (no petrol in those days), the poor horses could not stand up on the ice, so there was no chance of them pulling a cart. The result of this was that everyone had to do their best to get supplies. For example: us kids had to go down to the railway siding in Globe Road with our handmade cart to purchase a bag of coal for our Mums. This came straight off the coal trucks with the men shoveling it into bags. They could only bring it in as far as the siding.

Our handmade cart was just that, but nevertheless our pride and joy. It was made up of a long sturdy plank of wood with a large box nailed onto one end, and a set of pram wheels at each end for the mobility. One pair fitted under the box end on its long bar, the other pair fitted at the front end on a swivelling piece of wood to give the steering controlled by pieces of rope secured from either side of the swivel. This was decorated in different colours and designs. It would normally be raced around the streets at breakneck speed in competition with other carts. But for now a more serious use was called for, and they proved to be a boon, even if the bags of coal did bend a few of our axles! Can you picture in your mind boys with a heavy load trying to keep it upright and sliding about on the ice in the bitter cold? Then picture the runny noses and frozen fingers. We were determined Mum would have a nice fire that night.

The time, and the situation, educated children into becoming more and more expert at making their own toys. The materials for which, were easily obtainable from the various bomb sites all around. Not only were they able to put together the go-carts already mentioned and perfecting them, the next best project was the wooden scooter. This was made of the following component parts: two, one metre planks with a vee cut out of one end on both of them, to take steel roller bearing wheels; two blocks of wood; four screwed eye bolts and a long bolt to go through them to swivel. All put together and decorated, and milk bottle tops nailed on the front to form numbers. Great fun for the kids to fly around on, but they made an awful noise going over the paving stones.

The next thing on the list of 'must have' was collecting shrapnel. This was produced from the shells that were fired at the enemy planes. The shells would explode at a pre-determined height hoping to splatter the planes with shards of metal in an attempt to bring them down. One result was that the twisted shards fell back to earth, and if they didn't kill anyone in the process, they were eagerly collected by small hands to show off to friends, or to swop for even more twisted lumps of metal.

Other things revered were American comics and English comics. We would spend hours with friends swopping the ones they had not read. At one time I had in my collection a pile of 'Magnet's', these were the 'Billy Bunter of Greyfriars' comics. I only wish I had them now as they would be worth a tidy sum.

One of the fondest memories I have of that year were the times when all the family managed to get together, circumstances allowing. Particularly when we had Sunday tea, this would take place in our small kitchen, with Mum's oval table fitted into the bay window with a clean white tablecloth. There would be my three sisters, their two husbands, Mum and Dad and of course myself. The spread included: winkles, bread and a little butter, cake and jelly with Mum going around clutching a large pot of tea making sure all cups were kept full. On one occasion, Alice's husband Charles had previously been to America to join a ship that was on loan to England, and when they returned he brought with him food parcels from the States that contained tins of fruit and lots of nice things we had not seen for years. That Sunday we had a really good blowout. I can still hear the banter and laughter going on around that table, for these were nervous times and everybody made the best of things in every way no matter how small.

So onwards into 1944 where things took a turn for the worse. Now Germany was on the run, and being pushed back on all fronts. This situation had made them very desperate prompting them to turn to the terror weapons they had managed to perfect. There were two: the first being the V1 or more commonly known as the flying bomb. This as you may know was a pilotless aircraft with a bomb in its nose, programmed to run out of fuel over a pre-determined target. I saw a good many of these. When the engine stopped as it was above you, a terrifying feeling overwhelmed you that your time was up. On one occasion, it very nearly was. I was walking in Grove Road near my school, when one fell in the next street blowing me off my feet! When I recovered and went into the bombed area I was surprised to see the dead people lying in the street, and felt very sad that they looked so undignified there all covered in dust.

There was a strange link here, for some time before this my sister Alice had managed to rent a basement flat in Grove Road the other end to where this incident happened. It was to be her first real home for her husband and baby Carol. All the family pitched in to decorate and 'posh it up'. Sister Edna was to stay with them until Charles came home on leave. They moved in, and on the very first night, the very first flying bomb fell outside totally wrecking the whole place. Thankfully they escaped without any injuries. I know it's a fact about the flying bomb for there is a blue circle plaque on the nearby railway bridge noting the occasion.

The second terror weapon was the V2. This was even more terrifying than the V1. It was in the form of a giant rocket that carried a very large explosive warhead. Once launched it would travel twenty miles into space, and then fall at the speed of sound on a selected target. One did not hear it coming as it was travelling faster than sound by the time it arrived. The first thing that happened was the tremendous explosion followed by a sound very much like a train going by.

Having had a bad scare with the V1 flying bomb, I was to have an even more serious one with the new V2. It transpired that due to the lack of facilities at my school Cranbrook, we had to travel down to Molem Street at Cambridge Heath Road to attend our weekly woodwork classes. This school was fully equipped, and I always enjoyed our lessons there. But on this particular occasion my number was very nearly up. For a V2 landed just across the road from the school, fortunately on a previously bombed site, so no one was hurt there. As it exploded with a roar we students reacted automatically and dived under our woodworking benches - luckily for us! All the glass fanlights collapsed from above, covering everything in masses of chicken wired shards of razor sharp glass. In the event, the school was fairly badly damaged and I cannot remember ever going back there for more woodwork, much to my regret.

This then was the shape of things. One day your school was there, next it was gone, but not without a cheer from the kids! There was one particular incident, that brought great sadness to Cranbrook, that was when a V2 fell on Totty Street, Bow and we lost about twenty schoolfriends on that occasion. It was only after the war that we were informed that the Nazis were trying to perfect the atom bomb. One can only imagine what would have happened had they succeeded and put them in the V2's. I am sure that England would have been annihilated. I do not think that people here today, living the comfortable lives they do appreciate the fact, that it is due to the efforts and dogged determination of the allies to stop those scientists from achieving their aims then, things would not look as good right now.

1945 the war was over and we had won! I can easily bring to mind the joy and great relief that the announcement gave to everybody. The population went wild, there were masses dancing and singing in the street, and all of our family that were present went up to the Embankment to see the firework display. That was a fantastic night, we all had to walk home to Bethnal Green, and I remember Edna walking most of the way in her bare feet.

My fourteenth birthday had arrived, and it was time to leave the sanctuary of school, and go out into the great wide world to learn how to earn a living. In fact a job had already been lined up for me in the factory where my Dad was employed, the same place that we used to shelter in during the war. The factory manufactured heavy steel meshes for underwater projects, and guards for machinery. The job I was assigned bore no relation to my size and ability. In other words, I was too small for the heavy tasks. After a while my failure to pull the heavy metal rods through the stamping machine at the correct intervals, earned me one too many kicks up the backside, I decided I'd had enough of that sort of treatment, as I thought the corporal punishment bit had been left back in school! So I quit that job a bit smartish, and as the wages were only two pounds ten shillings a week of which my Mum let me keep ten shillings I was sure I could do better, and I did.

I managed to secure a job as a plumber's mate at Ames Building Contractors in Sugar Loaf Walk, only one hundred yards from where I lived in Gawber Street. Those buildings have all gone now. But at one time there was a great variation of shops and businesses along Globe Road and Sugar Loaf Walk. The plumber that I was assigned to named Sid Butlin was without doubt a first class craftsman. There was a wonderful opportunity to learn all about the trade from his vast experience, and he was willing to pass it on, but his idea of a learning curve was peculiar, and sometimes quite cruel. My job was of course to assist him in every way. His tools had to be burnished until they shone. He would tell me in advance of the task we were to do that day. I would then have to pack the tools he needed, but when we arrived at the site and he found a tool missing then I would have to go all the way back to get it at my own expense. I didn't mind that so much as I was earning three pounds a week now. There was however a cruel streak in him; on one occasion when instead of watching him I watched in fascination a plasterer in the next room skimming effortlessly across the ceiling, I heard Sid say 'here' and I held out my hand, still looking at the plasterer, and Sid dropped a piece of red hot solder into my hand with the comment that he paid me to watch him, and not the plasterer. Another time as he was using a paraffin blow lamp in a confined space the oxygen was being used up and making the flame die so he swung the lamp back to the doorway to let the oxygen recover, and as I was standing close behind him

14

tending to his every need, he set my hair on fire! His only mumbled comment was that I would have to keep my eyes open. I had a hammer head thrown at me after it became detached I ducked in time and the hammer head took a chunk out of the wall. I laugh at it now, but could you imagine that sort of behaviour now? One job we had was at a mansion in Epsom, where a lead hopper head had broken away and fallen to the ground so a new one had to be made. After taking it back to the yard, Sid made a new one even to embossing the designs into the lead so it matched all the others. The clients were very pleased, it was great to watch him. During my time with him doing remedial plumbing jobs we would sometimes be sent to up market places as just mentioned and that was very pleasant. But then, taking the rough with the smooth we could get unpleasant ones.

The one that stands out most was when our services were required on a street of houses that were being refurbished in Brick Lane, Stepney. The street was sandwiched between the pickle factory and the railway lines, so with the stink of pickled onions and the thunder of the passing trains every five minutes put our skills to the test. One of the houses previously finished was occupied by a woman and her family and she looked as if she had leprosy. To say we were alarmed at going anywhere near her was justified but we carried out our task. Looking back now makes me wonder how I survived the ordeal without becoming ill. Our meal breaks were taken in a cafe in Brick Lane. A place that I can only describe now as a greasy spoon and shudder to think about. We would order dripping toast, the dripping would be scooped out of a large bowl, with brown jelly at the bottom. I can only imagine now at this present time, the amount of bacteria it contained.

Sadly for me Sid retired at the end of the following year, so I was once again in the market for another source of employment. It was not very hard in those post war days to find work, for the depleted workforce was not able to fill the jobs available. Nevertheless, with the help of a recently found friend, Terry Chanter, I was taken on at three pounds ten shillings a week at his place of employment. Things were looking up! The company manufactured stainless steel hangers for x-ray pictures. We had to sort out all the component parts and spot weld them together after all the production processes had been completed in the upper part of the building.

Terry became my best pal, I found in him a great spirit of adventure, our interests included joining the Lawrence Cycling Club, belonging to the Young Liberals Association, the Youth Club at the 'Camel' public house and the sea cadets. The last one was to stimulate the biggest adventure of my young life. We joined the cycling club after I had bought my first bike ever for five pounds. It was a secondhand one; and curiously it had a brass plate on the front with the manufacturers name C.W.S. which strangely enough are my exact initials. We had wonderful days, starting off with the club early on Sunday mornings; dressed in our cycling garb of simulated plus four trousers and peaked caps. One had to look the part. Our Sundays would take us on a twenty mile round trip; with a pre-determined stop for breakfast, lunch and tea. Wonderful summer days, with nowhere near the traffic on the road that there is today. Then there was the big camping idea we had. A small tent was borrowed from friends and off we went to camp for the night in Epping Forest. It actually went quite well, a nice spot was found, our tent was pitched, our tea was brewed and sausages cooked. Having swapped stories we turned in, but sleep did not come easily for the night was filled with unfamiliar noises. A deer took an interest in us by sniffing around the tent. In the morning we found out in the cold light of day that what we thought during the night felt like large plums on our sleeping bags, and on our hair, turned out to be very large slugs!

Our venture into politics took the form of becoming Young Liberals, which amounted to no more than giving support to the prospective Liberal candidate for Bethnal Green, by distributing leaflets and slogans. I cannot say that I was ever influenced by it all, I think the main attraction was the social club they operated. The other youth club we attended, was at the 'Camel' pub on the corner of Sugar Loaf Walk. It had been converted during the war to provide a venue for young people to go. It had all the usual functions; darts, ping-pong and woodwork carried out on the bar!

Joining the Sea Cadets came about when in conversation with friends about new interests. After finding out more of the details we presented ourselves at T.S. Dauntless requesting to join. Dauntless wasn't so much a ship, it was a rather large house in Charles Square, Shoreditch. It was a fabulous organisation run by very dedicated people as we were to find out during our time spent there.
Attendance two nights a week was required, and instructions on seamanship, knots and splices, recognition of naval ranks. We had drill with 303 Lee Enfield rifles, which seemed to be a little bit too large for us, but the thing we learned most of all was discipline! After a trial period when they decided we were the right sort of youths they wanted, we were accepted into their ranks and duly issued with a uniform. Now having your uniform and getting it to fit are two different things. We later found out through experience that it not only had to fit, but it had to be customised to look 'Tiddly', a naval term.

To look 'Tiddly' the cap had to be damped and contoured overnight with the aid of elastic bands! to form wavy edges. The blue jacket had to be split a little more at the front. The reason for this would be to allow an elastic band to be passed around your back, and secured with a safety pin to either edge of the opening. Thus allowing it to be pulled out in a U shape thus exposing our manly chests! Oh the vanity of it all. The blue jean collar bordered with three white stripes, representing Nelson's three great battles, was usually very dark blue when first issued. This had to be bleached a little bit to make it lighter. We could not have people thinking we had just joined could we? No we were old hands! Now the bellbottom trousers were the crowning glory, they had to be as wide as possible at the bottom, with seven creases laterally across each leg to represent the seven seas. And when you stood still your shoes would be obscured by the bell bottoms. This was all very 'tiddly', until it rained when they would get very wet and flap around your ankles until they were sore. It's strange how a uniform can change one, on two nights a week by donning our regalia, we were swaggering jolly jack tars, whistling at the girls but the rest of the week would be spent doing our menial tasks just waiting to act the part again.

Other activities at the Sea Cadet Corps were varied and always extremely interesting. There were the weekends when we would be transported down to Eel Pie Island on the River Thames to spend a night on an old air sea rescue launch. This was big time for us, and I cannot tell you in words the elation that it brought. Then we became eligible for summer camps taken at various naval bases. Terry and I went to H.M.S. Victory in Portsmouth, where we were introduced to navy life, given hands-on instructions on boat handling. Also we spent a lot of time at H.M.S. Deadulus at Lee-on-Solent. This was a Fleet Air Arm base. It was all great fun to youngsters like us and even more for at that base we were taken up flying for the first time in our lives. Needless to say the whole thing impressed us greatly, especially me, for I was determined that I was destined for the Royal Navy just as soon as I was allowed.

Two years had passed since the end of the war and in 1947 things were still on ration and the results of that time were still very much in evidence. Terry and I were still employed at the same factory for a considerable time, but our interests began to differ. He had a fascination for cars and learning how to weld. I for my part lost interest in the job we were doing and left to find new employment in the plumbing trade. After that we drifted out of our friendship. Terry eventually emigrated to Canada, where I am glad to say he apparently made a fortune by inventing stackable cages for transporting chickens in a relatively humane way so his early days learning the art of welding really paid off. As for myself, I did find employment in the plumbing trade and I settled down to learn as much as I could from the plumbers and like myself plumber's mates; great guys full of fun but nowhere in the same league as old

Sid Butlin. They were ex-servicemen having done a crash course to emerge as plumbers. Good luck to them. I did pick up a lot of skills, a lot by hands-on experience, and a lot by watching their mistakes. We nonetheless were employed at some very good jobs one being The British Museum and that one holds memories of working up the side of the building on a very wobbly mobile stage. The plumber and I were to remove an old cast iron soil stack and replace it with a more up-to-date version. That meant starting at a height of seventy or eighty feet, and working our way down by lowering the stage by means of ropes. A task that had me worried from start to finish. Just one slip and we would have been gone.

I was sixteen now and I already had a fair amount of experience of life under my belt. but now we were moving into overdrive. My interests had taken a different direction by now, and I had become fascinated by motorcycles. After a period of time it was not surprising that I had to have one much to the dismay of my Mum. She said they were death traps. I don't know what she would think of the monster bikes they have now. In those days the bikes were a little more mundane, lovely machines that you could very easily take to pieces and do your maintenance with pleasure. I scraped together enough money to put down a deposit on one that had taken my fancy, with the remainder to be paid off over two years. It was a B.S.A. 250cc, quite big enough for a beginner. Dad went with me to the dealers in Hackney Road, mainly to act as my guarantor and partly to see that I wasn't being ripped off. The bike was bought and they kindly delivered it to our house for me as of yet I was about to learn how to drive it.

My tutor for this purpose who volunteered his services, probably after witnessing my feeble efforts, was named James Johnstone. He lived in the other half of Gawber Street. The two halves being divided by Brierly Street, and slightly offset to each other. Jimmy was a casual acquaintance who attended grammar school so although we lived quite near to each other, our way of life was quite different. Nevertheless he was a good tutor and patiently instructed me to start the engine, pull in the clutch, select your gear and ease the clutch back in again very slowly. The balancing was the easy bit, it was the bits in between that were difficult to remember, and to gain enough confidence to travel more than a few yards. But the catalyst came when I forgot the instructions and let my clutch in too fast. In doing so it jerked my throttle hand, the engine roared and I was off down the road like a bullet out of a gun! The bike and I went up the kerb, and I only managed, by sheer luck to steer it between the wall and the lamp post. Funnily enough that shock had for some reason done me a big favour as I now had come to terms with the bike and after that I went from strength to strength until at last I was in a position to take my driving test which I passed first time.

Mum became a bit paranoid about me leaving an expensive bike out in the street, and insisted that I should bring it indoors and put it in the front room. She went on so much that at last we agreed to do it, even after we explained to her the dangers of having petrol inside the house. After doing that for half a dozen times, resulting in knocking the paint off the doors and tearing the wallpaper she relented and ceased to nag. I could understand why she felt that it would be stolen for it was the only vehicle in the street. That seems hard to believe now in this age, but it's true and I have photographs of our street completely devoid of cars or bikes. Anyway I no longer had to struggle to manoeuvre the machine indoors.

I really enjoyed that great feeling of freedom on that bike, and I travelled far and wide for petrol was one shilling and ninepence a gallon! There were a few hairy moments though. One when I had my current girlfriend on the pillion and I failed to see a rather large pothole in the road. The result was that she shot off the pillion and landed on my shoulders. There was no rear springing on this model. The same girlfriend's father used to complain bitterly about me starting it up at night on leaving after bringing her home. So I had to always push the bike to the end of the street to start for fear of upsetting him. Looking back I don't know why I bothered for she dumped me anyway. A couple of times I came off on the slippery granite cobbles that still abounded the streets at that time, but all in all I came to no harm and continued to enjoy myself.

I had now turned seventeen and had left the Sea Cadets some time before but still retained this burning ambition to join the navy. I discussed it at great length with Dad who at last agreed that if that is what I really wanted, then he would give his consent. But reminding me that it was to be likened to jumping off a cliff, once you step off it's very difficult to change your mind. So the ball was in my court, and my current friend Stanley Dietman, who incidentally was also a member of the Sea Cadet Corps, and like me was eager to join the navy. He was slightly older than me, in fact nearly eighteen.

We took ourselves off to the Royal Naval Recruitment Office, in Tottenham Court Road They were very glad to see us and after filling in our application forms, we were told to return a week later for out physical and mental examinations. There was also a method in our madness, for we knew that when we reached the age of eighteen we would have to do two years National Service anyway, so this was one way of making sure we could join the service we most desired, even if it meant serving a longer term, and how! Our appointment for the medical was kept, and they were very thorough, tapping the knees, peering at everything, making copious notes. The mental exam consisted of solving written problems by multiple choices. Such as where you would put a load on a wheelbarrow, middle or either end. The results of the exam were good for us, and we were informed that we were suitable candidates. Now for the length of service. The Chief Petty Officer told us that the two options were seven years service with five years on reserve but as there wasn't any vacancies for that, the only option for us was twelve straight years continuous service. Being young and a little foolish, we both jumped at the chance. On reflection, not all that foolish, for I never regretted a moment of my navy career.

After the acceptance things began to move quite quickly, and we were to be enlisted the following month. In actual fact my pal Stanley went before I did, as I had lied a bit about my age and they had found out about it. In actual fact I was only seventeen and a half. I was told that if I went in then, the six months until I was eighteen would not even count, as the correct age to enlist was eighteen! But I agreed to the extra time, so the die was cast.

The next few weeks were full of mixed feelings, Mum was very upset at the thought of me going, as was the rest of the family. I was still in the plumbing business and the last place I worked was the St. John Peel pub, opposite Liverpool Street Station and looking out of the pub's window I would see uniformed personnel going in and out of the station, and thinking to myself that I'd be one of them soon. Little did I know what I had to go through to be as good as they obviously were.

Now for a Life of Adventure

I arrived at the recruitment office on time as I had been instructed. I was a bit overwhelmed by the sight of so many other candidates, as I had it fixed in my mind that I was to be the only one. This was lesson one, the navy never does things by half. As far as I remember there were about forty in the group. After all the formalities had been gone through, we were shipped off by train to a shore base; H.M.S. Royal Arthur. On arrival we were told that we had forty-eight hours to reconsider our position. If we decided to stay after that time we would be enlisted in the navy proper. If we decided to go then we would have to pay our own fare home. Well of course I stayed, but I think a few had a change of heart and left.

Royal Arthur was a large transit camp, where new recruits were kitted out and given preliminary drill instructions and then sent off to the various training ships or shore bases.

I was assigned to H.M.S. King George V or more affectionately known as K.G.V. I was extremely excited on the way down to Portland to join my training ship thinking how great it would be to actually sleep on a ship. My excitement would have been a little less if I had known what was in store for me. We arrived on the quay at Portland Harbour early afternoon, and on reflection we looked a comical bunch, with our ill-fitting uniforms, and laden down with heavy kitbags full of recently issued items of kit. Our hammocks should have been lashed up in a long sausage with the lashing rope done in seven evenly spaced half hitches. The inexperience showed for most of the hammocks were poorly done which meant that they came undone during the journey down leaving the thin mattress and pillow poking out of the gaps. I have no doubt that the people who worked in that area had seen the same sorry sight on a number of occasions before, so did not show any sign of surprise.

A boat transported us to K.G..V. that was moored in the harbour, I thought it looked big from the quay, but that was nothing compared to close up. The ship was enormous, it had a 36,000 ton displacement. Which meant that once in the water it displaced 36,000 tons of water. The guns main armament was capable of firing shells 15 inches in diameter and weighing one ton, for twenty miles! This then was the great K.G.V. one of the last big battleships that had fought so many sea battles in World War II as I was well aware after hearing of their exploits many times on the radio as a youngster.

We were then herded with our heavy loads up the gangway and onto the upper deck, and drawn up into a line where we were informed that we were the most horrible looking bunch of people they had ever seen. It had begun! This was the start to the procedure of breaking us down from what we were, to what they wanted us to be. After this point it became obvious to us that it was going to get a great deal worse. Our next move was to be shown the messdeck where we were to live and given a map to help us find our way around the ship. Also instructions on how to sling our hammocks. At this point I would like to explain the attributes of that wonderful invention, the hammock. For except on the odd times I resided in barracks, I spent the whole of my twelve and a half years using the hammock for my nightly rest. It consisted of a strong canvas sheet, approximately six feet six inches long, by four feet six inches wide. At the ends there were twenty four brass eyelets, into which went the same number of hemp light strands of rope; 'nettles'. They in turn were fixed through a large iron ring, and that in turn had a three foot length of sisal rope spliced onto it. These 'nettles' were of course the means of hanging, 'slinging' your hammock onto the hammock bars that were fixed to the ceiling, 'deck-head'.

The other essentials were, a thin mattress, pillow sheet and blanket the optional bit was two pieces of wood, each with a V cut into each end. These would fit into the nettles and hold the hammock open to a reasonable eighteen inches. The procedure for slinging your hammock would be to secure each end to the appropriate bars, so placed to bring it in line with the bow and stern of the ship. Adjust the ropes so that there was just a slight sag, then the blanket would be draped over it followed by the sheet. To get in you would grasp one of the bars, swing your legs up and drop them in first to steady your hammock, then drop the rest in. Wrap the sheet around you then the blanket and there you are, nicely cocooned, ready for dreamland in your own little oasis, free from the movement of the ship. Gravity enables the hammock to stay still while the ship moves around it. There is no need to explain what a boon that was.

In the morning the reverse would be to lash up your hammock in a long sausage and stand it in the hammock netting. That being the space provided to stow them out of the way until required again. After having been shown how to sling our hammocks we were then instructed that we would be awoken at 6.30am to start our first chore of the day scrubbing the upper deck. This would last for half an hour, followed by intensive activity to wash and shave and have breakfast by 7.45am ready for the day's instructions. Nothing prepared us for the next morning! Instead of having Mum calling you gently saying 'come on now you will be late', this was replaced by a Petty Officer wielding two dustbin lids crashing them together and at the same time roaring profanities at us in a terrifying way. This certainly had the desired effect of turning us into a bunch of frightened rabbits. After lashing up our sorry looking hammocks, we were herded onto the upper deck where we had to remove our shoes and socks roll our bellbottom trousers up grab a stiff broom and step out onto the wooden deck, by that time awash with icy cold sea water being liberally hosed by a sea booted and warmly clothed Petty Officer.

A line was formed and we had to scrub 'for'ard', towards the bow end of the ship; stop when told, turn about and scrub 'aft', rear end of the ship. This went on for half an hour by which time we were blue from the cold. It was only January and a nasty one at that. It was a mad rush after that to get below for a wash and for those that needed it a shave and of course breakfast. We came to know the coarse navy terms for the different types of breakfasts very quickly. Kippers were known as 'Spithead pheasants'; eggs bacon and tomatoes were known as 'Train Smash'; kidneys as 'Piss Strainers'; and probably the worst of all individual steak and kidney puddings as 'babies heads'. So you can see using navy terms was akin to using a different language altogether.

As the weeks went by we became hardened to the early morning scrubbing and the manic activities to get ready to be taught all the necessary lessons needed to become an ordinary seaman! The whole course lasted six months, after which I was to be sent to barracks to train in a specialist course. It wasn't all classroom stuff, there was a lot of hands-on learning to be done. At one point however they sent us in turn, to spend a day at sea on a frigate which was a very much smaller ship than the K.G.V. Needless to say there was a lot more movement. I was given the job of painting one of the many lobbies with one of the regular crew members who while we were painting went on and on about food, I think he took a delight in seeing the different colours that I was turning. In the end sea sickness got the better of me and I made a mad dash for the toilets, 'Heads'. I made it okay, but as I went head down in the pan to be sick, my hat shot off into the pan where I emptied my stomach straight into my hat!. The rest of the day was spent in extreme discomfort.

We also had very exciting times; for the K.G.V. was going to sea on a visit to the Channel Islands, and Bordeaux in France. By this time, into our fourth month of training we were beginning to look a little bit more presentable as our uniforms had been nipped and tucked to make them fit a little better. When we were allowed ashore in Guernsey I was doing my imitation of a real sailor, echoes of the sea cadet days. As it was not long after the previous occupation by the Germans it was interesting to see the results of that occupation. The massive gun emplacements and all the other paraphernalia erected on the coastal areas to resist any attempts of a landing. Of course the allies never did. They simply went around them. We enjoyed the visit, and the population seemed very pleased to see the young sailors to be! This would be a good time to explain that the ship was operated by the regular ships crew, while our role was to assist them, as part of our ongoing training.

The next port of call was Bordeaux. All this was completely new to most of us who, like me, had never been further than Southend. We soaked up the atmosphere like blotting paper soaks up ink!. My venture ashore there found me in one of those typical French bistro kind of places, right down to the tinny squeeze box music being played. Bordeaux being the place associated with wine, it wasn't surprising to find it to be very cheap, a fact that I was to make the most of!

I sat at the bar drinking glass after glass of vin rouge feeling quite merry but not drunk or so I thought. It was only when on the advice of the older crew members, that I should return to the ship, as being under age I was only allowed ashore until 10pm. As soon as I got outside I felt the effects of the wine when the fresh air hit me I was violently sick in the gutter. What a sight I must have been. You can almost imagine the passing people shaking their heads and muttering under their breaths. Two of the crew took charge of me and escorted me back to the ship making sure that I straightened myself up before we went up the gangway because it was an offence to return to the ship in a drunken state.

I remembered through the haze on the way back seeing those tram lines that run along the sea front with the trams running right past the ship. So it seemed to make sense a couple of days later when I heard the story about one of the crew 'gone adrift', returned late. When he was brought before the Captain to explain himself he said that as he was coming back to the ship on time his shoe managed to wedge itself in one of the tramlines. Well, he dragged his foot along the tram line, hoping to get opposite the ship where he could call for help but just before he could reach the ship the tram line diverted in another direction, so he had to follow that one and that made him late in getting back on board. I never heard the result of his misdemeanour but I'm sure it gave everyone a good laugh and he probably got away with it for sheer cheek.

After our visit we returned to Portland Harbour to resume the training in earnest, we were made to box and swim and do physical exercise. I think the worst were the kit musters once a month. On these occasions your kit had to be laid out on your spare hammock, cleaned and shining exactly as in the instruction poster, perfectly in line and perfectly in size. If it failed the muster you would have to do it again a few days later. I can tell you we spent some late nights getting it right. Sometimes the inspecting officer would hurl an offending piece as far as he could while you looked on sheepishly hating him.

There was a light at the end of the tunnel now, for the training period was reaching its conclusion. We were very shortly going to qualify as ordinary seamen. Naturally the interest in our appearance had undergone a certain amount of change. And we all wanted to look 'tiddly', well I mean, isn't that what we joined the navy for? To catch the eyes of the girls, and make our Mums' proud of us? I did have one embarrassing moment on the question of dress, and it happened when I was on a week's leave while I was still training. It was the norm in the Sea Cadet days to bleach your blue jean collar to a more acceptable colour. Well, while on leave I decided to do the same thing, the only trouble was that I put too much bleach in and I left it overnight. The result was that in the morning I had a shock when I saw I had a very near white collar! On returning to the ship, and removing my overcoat for the inspection of returning liberty men, I was the object of laughter when they saw my white collar. The inspecting Chief Petty Officer roared 'Ooh look we have a Mediterranean sailor here' the implication was that it was a sun bleached sea going and timed served one. To help us achieve our desire to look 'tiddly', was the naval tailor 'Bernards'. Their representative had free access to the ship, to measure people up for their 'tiddly' suits that you could buy on the never~never. Usually he came after the working period, and as he came into the messdeck, he would call out 'here comes Robin Hood', when everyone would shout in reply, 'Robin Bastard'.

The suits when made would be very tight fitting. And needed the help of another person to get out of the jacket. This was done by bending over, crossing your arms and placing your hands on the persons hips, who would then get the bottom of the jacket and pull it over your head. This was an exercise so widely used amongst us that no words were used to implement it, you automatically did it for your friends 'oppos'. There was a downside to these suits for when one rode on a bus, the bumping and jolting in these tight garments tended to arouse unwelcome feelings in the lower regions. Well we were young and virile! It would be quite noticeable when we got up to leave, for those particular parts would be at eye level to the other passengers, so we had to cover our modesty by putting our caps over the offending part until we left the bus, where we could adjust our dress!

I have written a lot about uniforms and this is to put into perspective how important it was for us. One doesn't see them worn in public very much now because of the wearers being targeted. Nonetheless note the natty attire worn by Stanley Dietman and myself.

The great day arrived when we finished our training and we qualified as ordinary seamen. I was drafted to Chatham Barracks on the 28th June 1949. This was to be my home base and whilst there I did a course at gunnery school and became a 'Quarterer's Armourer', which in fact meant gun maintenance. This suited me fine as I had always been keen on a mechanical profession. Chatham Barracks was fine by me as well because it is only about twenty five miles from London and meant that I could get home more often.

The actual gunnery course was a great experience, it took me into another dimension of learning. It was both arduous and complicated for not only did we have to learn all the working parts but also how to operate every position on the different types of armament that ships carried. It was a myriad of things from hydraulics to setting fuses on the shells to explode at a certain height. I would not want to bore you with those details. The whole course was for six months.

I finished my gunnery training on the 3rd of February 1950, and was surprised that two weeks later I had been drafted to H.M.S. Swiftsure. That meant a journey up to Invergordon in Scotland. I was greatly surprised, and pleased, that on arrival I found out that my 'oppo' Stanley was also a member of the ship's

Stanley Dietman and myself

26

company. It's always nice to see a friendly face. H.M.S. Swiftsure was a county class cruiser. This meant that she was about half the size of the old K.G.V. but just as powerful and twice as fast. They were built for just that purpose, to bridge the gap between the very large and smaller ships. My allotted job on her was very grandly titled 'Optical Artificer's Assistant'. Our duties were to maintain the binoculars, large and small The large ones were in the gun direction tower, at the very top of the superstructure. These were enormous binoculars that stuck out from either side of the tower, and used. to track ships at a great distance. It was very strange that the artificer always wanted to test these only when we were in harbour. We always managed to focus on the windows of the surrounding houses. I can tell you, some of the things we saw were quite interesting to say the least. The opticals were so powerful the illusion was that you were in the same room as the unsuspecting persons.

Apart from the binoculars our other duties included looking after the transmitting table. This table was in fact a mechanical computer. On top of the table were lots of handwheels that fed in, when operated, the wind speed, enemy course and speed and other various information and quite mechanically would give the angle and direction to fire your shells in front of the enemy ship, so that they both meet at the same point. Kerpow! The Swiftsure had a very distinguished career. In fact the surrender of Hong Kong by the Japanese was signed on board her. She was the flag ship of the fourth cruiser squadron in the Pacific in 1945, so you can see that I was in good company.

In the coming months I was quite happy aboard this ship with the exception of an incident which concerned the loss of two shipmates. This happened whilst showing the flag in Devon just before Christmas. These two young Royal Marines had been ashore, got plastered on scrumpy, and on returning managed to lock themselves in the gun room and being completely incapable laid on their backs and choked on their own vomit. What a tragic affair for their families.

There was a second tragic accident shortly afterwards whilst on exercise with the home fleet. Our ship was acting as escort and the R.A.F. were the attacking force. After one run past the ship the aircraft did a loop the loop but the pilot misjudged the height and hit the water where he was killed instantly. As I looked over the ship's side I saw his body float past. Divers went over the side to recover his body but were unable to do so. There were also one or two other incidents but nothing too serious thankfully.

Our travels took us around the coast of England on goodwill visits and at one point the Swiftsure visited Sunderland where I met a very nice girl. Our romantic interlude was short lived for the ship only stayed for a few days but not before we made arrangements for me to spend one week of my forthcoming two weeks leave with her at her family home. The plan was for me to have one week at home and one week at her house. I managed to get my railway warrant from the navy, made out to Sunderland instead of my home address so we were all set. But disaster struck; for during my first week at home I lost my wallet in the cinema. No one returned it, even though they could obviously see who it belonged to. The trip to the girl's home was off, as well as the railway ticket as all my cash had gone too. I wrote to her to explain, but to no avail as I never heard from her again. So there I was, a whole week in front of me with no money and nothing to do. But all was not lost, for I had read in the paper that owing to an influenza epidemic there was a shortage of staff at the Bethnal Green hospital to deal with the rush of patients. That gave me ideas, and I took myself along to the hospital and volunteered my help. I was interviewed by the Matron, who was quite pleased with the offer. She told me I would not be paid, but I would be fed. They issued me with a white coat and told me to report to the Staff Nurse at a particular ward. I felt quite elated walking along the corridors, nodding at people who looked as if they thought I was a doctor. The Staff Nurse soon put me to work helping the regular nurses but I was surprised when she gave me the task of giving one patient a bath! To do this she explained; I had to remove these tubes from the connections in his side, put the rubber plugs in where the tubes had been, and then bathe him in the bathroom. She said that I must remember the plugs for without them he would sink, she said with a laugh. After a couple of days, she was shocked to find out that I was not a provisional male nurse as she thought I was, but a sailor. After that I was given more menial jobs, but I must say that I thoroughly enjoyed the experience.

My service on board the Swiftsure came to an end on the 30th April 1951, when I returned to Chatham barracks to await another gunnery course, but until I started it I was put into the barrack guard. Dressed up in my white belt and gaiters, armed with a chrome tipped baton guarding the barrack gates, I thought I was the bee's knees. This guard was always drawn from ratings awaiting other ships, or like me courses. We were in fact the back up for the regular naval police, who incidentally had the unlovely nickname of 'The Crushers'. The correct name was Regulating Staff, who were known for their stubborn devotion to duty, and their unrepentant way of knocking seven bells out of wrongdoers should they resist their attentions, ha ha!

Our duties would be to guard the main gates on a shift system. One of my favourite gates was St. Mary's, for this was the W.R.N.S. entrance. The girls were not allowed to stay out all night without

28

permission. If they were late coming back 'adrift', they would try and climb over the wooden gate, but the Petty Officer in charge tied tin cans on the gate which would rattle as soon as the gate was touched. When it happened he would jump up shouting 'Another one for the guardhouse' I think he had been there too long.

Once again though, tragedy was just around the corner, waiting to catch up with me. On one particular night, when I was on duty on the main gate as barrack guard we, and medical staff were sent up the approach road to the barracks to attend an incident. When we arrived to our horror there were a lot of injured and dead Royal Marine cadets lying everywhere. We had to assist the medical staff running messages, collecting stretchers, blankets etc, etc. What had happened was that the cadets were marching down to the barracks for some instructions but those in charge of them had committed the fatal error of not having a warning light at the rear of the marching body. They were also not marching facing the oncoming traffic. There was a very high wall on either side of the approach road, making it very dim. A bus came down the road behind them and hit the marchers before he could stop. There were a lot of recriminations after that terrible incident, and I heard that the bus driver never seemed to get over it.

There were some funny sides to the job. In the morning watch on the main gate, I had to walk along the terrace road that bordered the parade ground. On this road were a number of wooden figureheads, that used to grace the bows of the old warships. Some had hands outstretched with a finger pointing the way forward. Some cleverdick, on his way back from having a good drink ashore would stick a contraceptive on the outstretched finger! In the end this little joke became so annoying that they had the 'Chippie' carpenter along to cut off the hands!

By this time I had bought my second motorcycle, I sold the first one when I joined the service. This latest one was also a B.S.A. 250cc, and this allowed me to visit home quite often.

Another incident in 1951 was the flooding of Canvey Island. I was not involved with this affair, but lots of the lads were drafted off to help out with rescuing and trying to sand bag up the breaches in the sea defences. Quite a lot of the island people lost their lives in these floods I am sorry to say.

Femme Fatale

By this time I had re-entered the gunnery school to do my second course for my second class rating. While there, as usual, one made friends with classmates and A/B Ernie Hay and I had quite a lot in common so we became the best of 'oppos', as in opposite number, and on occasions would spend weekends at each other's homes. While we were at my home, we decided to spend the evening at a pub called the 'Rising Sun'. This particular pub was quite famous in the East End of London for its entertainment. One of the acts was the 'Singing Cowboy'. He would be dressed up in all the cowboy gear but not only that, he would bring his white horse in the bar as well which stood there quite calmly while he did his act! As far as I can remember it never disgraced itself once. On this particular night, as we left the pub just on closing time, we spotted two young ladies across the road. After the preliminary whistling, we nipped across to introduce ourselves. They told us 'a bit coyly' that they were Pat and Iris Callow. Chatting and joking we walked them to their home in Ellesmere Road, Bow.

When we arrived at number '71' there seemed to be a party going on. The music was quite loud and there was a man helping a woman down the stairs at the front door saying 'Look, my old woman, pissed again'. I am not sure what Ernie thought but it crossed my mind that this was a madhouse.

We were invited in, the piano was going hell for leather, and the people were quite obviously enjoying themselves dancing up and down. It wasn't the only thing going up and down, for as Ernie pointed out to me, you could see the floorboards going up and down by the mark left on the skirting boards. Apparently these parties occurred on most Saturday nights in alternate houses after the pubs closed. A couple of crates of beer would be bought in the pub before closing time and taken off to the respective house where the party would be held. I saw on one occasion the piano taken out of the front room of '71', and carried by a number of men, 'a bit worse for drink', up the street to the next party house who were lacking a piano. When they arrived there, it was impossible to get it into their front room so it was plonked down in the passage where the player could tinkle away!

Pat and Iris had two younger brothers, Eric and Colin, their Dad 'Bill' was in the bookmaking business. I remember him sitting in the front room of '71' surrounded by betting slips and money balancing on every bit of space and a cigarette constantly in his mouth with long ash hanging from it.

Someone would always go over to him, with an ashtray, and tap the cigarette underneath so that the ash would fall into the tray. Their Mum 'Alice' was a worldly wise person who could deliver a very profound answer to a question with more than a trace of humour.

Ernie was quite taken with Pat and continued to date her while Iris and I didn't reign for long, as it seemed that we were not cut out for one another. I must admit that I did rather fancy Pat! She was a surprising person, and was fascinated by the navy. She had a cupboard full of naval magazines! But there you are, she was going out with Ernie.

Ernie and I finished our course, and shortly after he was drafted off to H.M.S. Cheviot, and went off to do a two year commission in the Far East. It's frightening to think of it now, but that's how long you were sent away on commission, two years at a time. I was drafted to H.M.S. Armada and my destination was to the Mediterranean Fleet at Malta for two years.

I joined 'Armada' on the 11th of December 1951 at Chatham Dockyard. She was a battle class destroyer built in 1943 and served in the Pacific until 1947 so once again I was in honourable company. First we had to do a work-up period, which meant, putting to sea for the purpose of everyone getting used to their respective jobs by doing repeated practice, over and over again until perfect. The whole ship was worked, from guns to seamanship, to the engine room. Once all was satisfactory, we sailed for our departure point of Portland Bill which seemed to be the traditional departure venue. Now we were on our way, and did not expect to see our families until two years later, so you can imagine that was an extra hurdle we had to come to terms with. The 'Armada' was a good old ship, that had seen a fair amount of action in its time. So it was no surprise that we began to find out it did have a lot of faults; they were to become apparent when we hit bad weather, which we did on reaching the Bay of Biscay which is renowned for that.

The first thing we did in bad weather was fix the gun turrets in a 'fore and aft' position, then there was a pneumatic rubber tube that had to be inflated around the bottom of the turret to prevent any sea water getting through. The only trouble was, that our tube on the for'ard gun was perished and could not be inflated. As that turret was above our mess deck we frequently got flooded. Sometimes you would get up in the morning to find that there was a foot of water swirling about, and floating in the water would be socks and underpants which would be blocking up the inlet for the pumps that were carrying the water away. I must admit, it wasn't always like that, for we probably had more good days than bad.

In addition, we had some very bad rust in places less accessible, and a couple of bulkheads that were panting in bad weather. This meant that these bulkhead's 'steel partitions' had bulges in them, and when the ship was rolling, they would crack from one side to the other, with a sound like a gun going off. So you can imagine, the old ship was looking a bit sad but I can assure you that after some months of hard work, driven on by the Petty Officers, 'Captains of the Tops' she looked a treat, and we all became very proud of her.

Having overcome the bad weather in the Bay, we arrived at the beginning of the Mediterranean, Gibraltar. We were to stay there for a short while to recuperate before continuing to take up our station in Malta. Gibraltar is a fascinating place; absolutely chock-a-block full of history. Seized by the British a long time ago, we turned it into a fortress with miles of tunnels carved out inside the rock. Massive structures that housed a hospital, barracks and water supplies gathered from the outside faces of the rock. Being completely self-sufficient, it was never to be taken, not by Napoleon, the Spanish or Germans.

So this was the furthest point that young Charles had ever been and as soon as I was allowed, I stepped ashore to sample the delights of 'Gib'. The first thing that became apparent, was the shops. The main street was lined with them, displaying goods that only existed in my imagination, it was just like Christmas.

To buy anything one had to haggle a great deal. We soon found out that was the way things were done here, so when I spotted a wonderful looking figurine purported to be a Tibetan monk, I engaged with the shopkeeper in a prolonged haggle. I finally bought the figurine for 'one pound', much to the amusement of my accompanying 'oppos'. I still have him today in safe keeping after fifty-six years! I did have him valued some years ago at Sotheby's, and they arrived at a figure of 'four hundred pounds' Not a bad profit on a pound. I would not sell him now for he is like one of the family. My Mum had him for some time sitting in her front window in Gawber Street, and having seen some children staring at him from outside, she overheard them say 'Cor, he don't half look like my teacher!' I must add that the figurine was quite ferocious looking.

The little bars that were dotted along the main street were good fun. But they paled into insignificance when compared to one establishment called 'The Winter Gardens'. This place had a very large bar, with a stage, and on this stage, young ladies performed Flamenco dancing. It was fantastic in our novice eyes. With their Spanish dresses, black shiny hair, and castanets clicking away. All the young sailors were naturally mesmerised by the sight. These girls were from across the border, and lived in a place called La Linea. This being the last Spanish town, before you arrived in Gibraltar.

When the girls were not dancing, they circulated among the young sailors, encouraging them to buy drinks for them. These drinks were no more than coloured lemonade, but at very inflated prices, for which the girls received a commission. More drinks, more commission. The drinks had to be soft, because at the rate the ladies consumed them, had they been anything else the girls would have fallen off the stage at regular intervals. As it was, the only danger they seemed to be in was visiting the toilet too many times. One of the girls took quite a shine to me, sat chatting in awkward English, in between her dancing numbers. In the end she asked if I would like to see her home!

Of course I agreed, and at the end of the evening we left the building. She insisted that it was necessary to go by taxi. When the taxi was found, the driver wanted paying upfront for the fare. After that was done, off we went. Being unfamiliar with the area, I wasn't sure where we were going, until I realised that we were at the Spanish border, and I was ordered out of the taxi.

The police were asking me for visa papers. By that time the taxi had taken off, with its lady occupant laughing and waving out of the back window. Ah well. They say that there is one born every minute, and they are so right for no one was allowed across the border without a visa. I wonder if she knew that, ha ha!

After our short stay at Gibraltar we departed for the last of the journey to Malta. It was not the last time we were to visit 'Gib' for on occasions it was to become like our second home. The trip through the Mediterranean was a bit rough as it was still January, but on arrival the weather had changed, and the sun was shining and had turned altogether very pleasant. Our final destination was to be Sliema Creek, alongside Manoel Island. This was the berthing place of the Third Destroyer Squadron. Unknown to us, the squadron was having its regatta that very day, so it was with amazement as we entered harbour that we saw what looked like pirates everywhere in boats. Once we were safely secured to the buoy, they started to raid us, and we were ordered to turn the hoses on them in retaliation. Then one of the pirate boats fired a brown smoke bomb, from a Verey pistol and that went through an open port hole into the officers mess!

I liked the new atmosphere of belonging to a seasoned squadron, whose job it was to travel around the Med. on what was called 'goodwill visits' showing the flag. But seen by most as a slightly menacing warning of the strength of the Royal Navy.

After our riotous, and hilarious, introduction to Malta, we began to settle down to our new way of life. The only odd thing was the catering arrangements on the 'Armada'. Normally, navy ships would cook the daily meals, and serve the respective mess decks with their quota in large trays, to be dished out on plates in the mess. But our catering was on a 'Canteen Messing' arrangement. This meant that each mess was allowed so much money a day. The N.A.A.F.I. shop on board, that was run by two Maltese N.A.A.F.I. staff, held all the food requirements in the store and refrigeration units on the ship. The mess decks would appoint two members of the mess to act as cooks for the week, who would think of the meals that everyone would agree to. Then they would order the ingredients from the canteen. Not with cash, but with an order book. Then the two cooks of the week would prepare the food to be cooked by the chefs in the ships main galley. It all seems very complicated trying to explain it here on paper, but after a certain amount of practice it worked well enough, and gave us the chance to have food that we liked. It all depended on the cooks of the week, some had very funny ideas about food.

On one occasion myself being cook of the week, I thought it would be nice if the lads had some nice mince pies. Even though I followed the instructions for making flaky pastry things went wrong when they were cooked. They went rock hard, and the lads finished up throwing them at one another, they made quite a bang when they hit the bulkheads! Another of my specials was a hot pot with boily bakes. These were dumplings that would be soft underneath and baked on the top. The only trouble was that an error in the ingredients led me to use self raising flour in the dumplings! During the cooking process, I had an urgent call from the chefs, for the boily bakes had grown to a tremendous size and were lifting the top of the pot off. I put that one down to the learning curve. One of the drawbacks of following the previous cooks of the week, was to find that someone had purchased a hundred fags on the strength of the order book and that meant you had to economise on that week's allowance to square the book up.

Being the cook wasn't all bad though, for it meant that you were excused duties, to look after the mess, cleaning, washing up etc. It also meant that you didn't have to rush over breakfast when the rest of them were flying about to get ready to 'fall in' and detailed off for their days duties. One could relax have another cup of tea, another ciggy, great!

Like Gibraltar, Malta had been under British rule for centuries so it was not very surprising that English was almost their native tongue. This made life a lot easier from everyone's point of view. The people were a canny lot though. I could understand that seeing what they had been through during the siege in the Second World War. In fact the island as a whole received the George Cross for their valour. They had very nearly starved to death, as the ships were unable to get through with supplies. This was a fact that helped me understand my feeling of disbelief and shock at seeing some of the Maltese workmen employed to do jobs on the ship, picking through the food waste outside the galley for morsels of food. These were put in shiny stainless steel cans they all wore on their belts. I can only assume that it was a habit adopted during the war, and was still being carried on. Generally the population were very good, and very devout Roman Catholics.

Everything was tuned for the Services, the Royal Navy in particular, and when visiting Valetta the main town, all you could see, on walking up the main street, was a sea of sailors white hats bobbing up and down. Hundreds of them, no doubt seeking the evening's entertainment. The favourite haunt of all these matelots was a place called The Gut, the real name being Straight Street. This was situated right behind Government House. The Gut was lined either side with bars, and eating places. The bars with names like Morning Star, Bing Crosby Bar etc. were I admit pretty seedy and questionable but the music was loud and the Anchor beer was good.

The Morning Star had a lady singer, who sounded remarkably like Mirielle Matthieu, and they called her Little Sparrow. She would be accompanied by a gentleman playing a violin. And while singing, she would stand with her hand underneath his legs, holding on to his testicles, so every now and again, she would give them a squeeze, and make the player go right up the music scale until she eased off. This would always raise a great cheer from the audience. So that goes to show you the quality of the entertainment, doesn't it?

But going ashore to drink and make merry was not the only attraction. For Malta, like 'Gib', was full of history, from the Roman conquest onwards. Two of my favourite places were the Roman baths at Rabat, and the city of Medina, where the streets are only about four feet wide, and that excluded any traffic. That being so they call it the Silent City. There was the usual cinema, shops etc, and there was a very large N.A.A.F.I. Club on Manoel Island. That was a great venue, and on occasions variety stars would appear in a show that would be put on there.

As most ships were tied up to buoys out in the harbour, it was necessary to get a water taxi to be able to go ashore. These taxis; were called Dghajsa, which would always be circling the ships awaiting a fare. They were driven by a guy with a long oar at the stern. But when loaded with about six or seven matelots, who were in a hurry to get ashore for a drink, they would all roll their sleeves up, and use their hands like paddles so it looked for all the world like an Indian canoe shooting along, especially as the shape of the 'disos' was very similar to the Venetian gondola.

Once ashore we would continue the journey to Valetta by a horse drawn carriage called a 'gharrie'. These carriages were lovingly decorated and cared for. The matelots were still in a hurry, and gave the driver extra to get a move on. It was not unusual to see two 'gharries' racing up the road, side by side, with matelots hanging out of the sides, pretending to shoot at one another like in the Wild West. One story that circulated was that a number of matelots were up before the Captain, for being 'adrift' off leave, and were asked to explain themselves. The first one said that the 'gharrie' horse dropped dead and they had to walk back. The second one said the same thing. The captain said to the third 'I suppose your horse dropped dead?' but the third one said 'No I could not get by for dead horses'! There is always a joker.

The co-operation between the public and the Services was usually very good. But it did fall off a bit when after long negotiations, the dockyard workers decided to go on strike for more pay. Things really took a turn for the worse when they threatened to take over the dockyard after being turned down over their pay. That's when the Services were brought in. We were all fitted out with tin hats and long batons, and we all formed up on the different approach roads to the dockyard. The Services were out in strength, Army and Navy, but I am glad to say that the dockers took a good look at those massed ranks and realised they could not win. I was very grateful for the decision otherwise 1951 would have turned out a little bit more sad than it did.

Valetta harbour and dockyard had to maintain the Services during the strike. That was an essential necessity. That's when we all had to be used again for off-loading supply ships, attending incoming, and outgoing Naval ships and also working the tugs around the harbour. I think this is where 'Armada' drew the short straw for our job in this operation was to supply the personnel to refuel the tugs. The only problem was, that they were coal burners. After being fitted out with overalls, soft hats and gloves, we were transported down to the coaling jetty to face a huge mountain of coal, and to add to our agony we found out that the Maltese way of doing the job was for each man to fill up a wicker basket, sling it up on his shoulder, walk over to the edge of the jetty, and tip it into the coal barge. We found it impossible to lift those baskets, so we resolved to do it the easier way by filling all the baskets, and by grasping one handle in the front and the one behind, we made a long snake and in unison would pick them up and move off to the jetty's edge. Once the barge had been filled up this way, with tons of coal it would be taken out to circulate the tugs and refuel where necessary. This went on for a week or more until thank goodness the strike was settled. There is no need to explain how dirty and exhausting that job was. On returning to the ship for lunch breaks they would not allow us below, we had to stay on the upper deck and eat, then get hosed down when we returned at the end of the day! I will never know how those Maltese dockers could stand that job.

Although life seemed to return to normal after the strike there was a certain amount of tension. The Premier of Malta, Dom Mintoff, was anti-British, and very determined to get independence for Malta. Trouble loomed again when the local brewery decided to put up the price of Anchor beer. This was seen as a direct insult to the Services, as they were the people who consumed a lot of it, and there was no need for the rise. In retaliation, Lord Mountbatten, who was Commander of the Mediterranean Fleet, put Valetta and The Gut 'out of bounds' to all personnel. That meant a big loss to the bars and shops in that area. There was quite a strong naval police patrol to stop anyone breaking the curfew. Some were successful at avoiding detection but four ratings were chased, and three of them caught while the fourth one escaped by devious means and continued drinking in the empty bars. He, now the worse for drink, stupidly turned up at the naval patrol office, telling the Provost Marshal, who was in charge of the three other ratings in his cells, that he was their mouthpiece, and that he was there to spring them. So they sprung him right in alongside the others. Apart from that period, our routine was good. We travelled the 'Med' and visited fabulous places like; Monte Carlo, Nice, Tarranto, Sicily and many more.

Life was to change drastically during that year for trouble was brewing in Egypt, and eventually led to the abdication of King Farouk the ruler of Egypt. The following Saturday morning we were all put on a state of alert, and ammunition barges began to arrive alongside. There was a rush to fully ammunition the ship and we put to sea that night, still not being told why. After we were out of harbour, it was disclosed that we were on our way, with a group of ships to secure Tobruk. This was because French and English interests were being threatened by a take-over of the Suez Canal. The skipper ended the announcement by saying: We may be attacked by the Egyptian Air Force, so there may be blood for supper tonight!

By the time we arrived at Tobruk we had been kitted out with webbing, arms and ammunition and fully briefed on the landing that was to take place. So it happened, alongside the other ships forces we landed on the beach. I am very glad to say that there was no resistance.

The anticipation of the landing had been very nerve racking for us all, as none of us younger ones had experienced any sort of firefight. Luckily the only resistance we met was some arabs trying to sell us bits and pieces. 'Armada' didn't stay long at Tobruk I am glad to say, for it was a really creepy place taking into account the fighting that went on there. The water in the harbour was crystal clear, and you could see the sunken ships and all the debris of war laying on the bottom quite clearly.

Our next destination was to be Port Said, where we spent some time at Admiralty House, at the entrance to the Suez Canal. Our next duties were to escort convoys of ships travelling through the canal, one destroyer at the front of the convoy, and one at the rear. Sometimes we were fired at during our journey though only small arms stuff, which was returned with something a bit heavier. The French and English governments were determined to hang on to the canal. The routine was to escort the convoy through to the Bitter Lakes, whereas the convoy would carry on, and we would anchor there for the night, and pick up a convoy going back down the canal, the next day. Anchoring there at night made us more than a little bit vulnerable, so lights were rigged up all around the ship shining down into the water. Armed sentries were posted throughout the night, with instructions that the navy had no divers of any description operating, so anything seen moving in the water was enemy, and was to be fired upon, and at the same time, the alarm was to be sounded with whistles provided.

Unfortunately while on my shift, in the dim light beyond the glare of the floodlights I thought I saw a shiny black suit, and heard the rush of air as he broke surface. So I opened fire with my Lanchester, and blew my whistle. All hell broke loose. Searchlights were switched on, people shouting orders, only to reveal that I had just killed a porpoise!

After some weeks of these duties, we were relieved by another destroyer, and had to return to Malta. On arrival we played our signature tune on entering harbour, 'High Noon'. This was a tradition with the Third Destroyer Squadron, all ships had their own tunes, these tunes were always played very loudly over the loudspeakers on entering or leaving harbour. It was seen as a camaraderie gesture.

After the trials and tribulations at Suez we had a brief sojourn in Malta. It wasn't long though before we were engaged in an exercise with the American Fleet. This all took place in the 'Med'. It was all pretty boring at first acting as convoy escort, moving along at about eight knots for days on end; every now and again zooming around to repel mock attacks by the American submarines. The exercise ended, and we all berthed at Trieste harbour. It was an eye opener for us, because we were invited by the Yanks on board their ships to see films, and to visit the aircraft carriers; unbelievably huge.

The most pleasant surprise was when the British Army invited us for a long weekend. They were in a place called Klagenfurt in Austria. I was lucky enough to be chosen to go, travel was by means of a coach right through the Austrian Alps. To a novice that journey was quite frightening with the sharp narrow bends, and sheer drops for hundreds of feet. We eventually arrived to find that we were to be billeted in a former S.S. Gestapo camp. All this had been taken over by the British army of occupation. It was quite a weird feeling as we entered, for on either side of the gates was a statue of an S.S. Guard. Our consternation was soon dispelled, for after a meal we were invited by the army to a party around the camp's swimming pool. The dress to be worn, was swimming trunks. It was to be a novel sort of party as all the bottles of beer were lying on the bottom of the pool! If you wanted a drink you knew what you had to do. Do I need to illuminate that a few rescues were needed that night.

In the days to follow we naturally explored the town, and found the Austrians fairly amenable, except when visiting the bars, where the local men seemed to glare at us. Probably thinking; are these the servicemen who beat us? On one occasion, my 'oppo' and I, having had a fairly good drink and a stare in the local bar sat ourselves down on the kerb, hoping for a bus to take us back to the camp, when a guy in civvies came over and told us to get up on our feet, and make ourselves respectable, telling us he was Military Police. We let him know that we were Senior Service, and that he should bug off. He did but five minutes later a jeep load of red caps came roaring around the corner and took us into custody. In the soup again! But we did enjoy that break immensely.

An exercise that followed when we returned to Malta would involve one of our own ships acting as an enemy. It would steam off into the darkness, and the rest of the squadron try to find him, with all the technical aids that we possessed. Sometimes the chase would last for days and nights. If they were found at night, star shells would be fired to illuminate them. On one occasion during some heavy weather, we had been closed up, 'manning', in our turret for a number of hours due to the fact that we were on the trail of the enemy. The guns were switched to auto. That meant they were being controlled from the gun direction tower, which could move all the guns onto different bearings at the touch of controls. Having been shut up in the turret so long, it was hot and oily, and with the sea running as it was, one of the young loaders cocked his head over the gunwell to be violently sick. The gunwell is the space where the back end of the guns go, when they are elevated. So the very moment the lad's head went over, the guns started to elevate. I saw them move, and I hooked my foot under his neck and jerked his head out of the way. On seeing the guns whoosh past his face, that increased his sea sickness.

Just before Christmas we were astounded to hear that 'Armada' was to cut short its commission and return to Chatham. This was to facilitate putting the 'old girl' into reserve, and to pick up a brand new ship from the makers 'John Brown' in Clydeside, Glasgow.

So it was, in January 1953 we left Malta for the return journey to England. For us it was a sad and a happy occasion at the same time, for although we had made many friends, we were happy at the prospect of seeing our families again. As we left harbour we played our signature tune 'High Noon' which prompted the squadron to send a semaphore signal to us; 'Do not forsake us, oh Armada!' This time it was a bit more serious, for normally they would be firing potatoes at us from a makeshift cannon. I am quite sure they were all mad in that squadron. Good memories.

Our duties were not finished yet, for we were to escort home eight 'Mickey Mouses'. These being small wooden minesweepers. Wooden because they were used to clear magnetic mines during the war. Our job was to give them support back to the U.K., and leave them at Southampton, to be placed in mothballs until they were needed.

The journey home was eventful, for after a short stay in 'Gib', we continued around the corner of Spain and into the Bay of Biscay. Here we ran into one of the worst storms of the year. It took us three days to get through it. Three days I shall never forget. The conditions were bad enough for us, but devastating for the 'Mickey Mouses'. We lost two of them in the storm, and sustained a lot of damage when rescuing the crews from those two ships. They were simply overwhelmed by the weather and water and sank.

Very sadly we lost one of our crew over the side. The 'Armada' was fitted with walkways well above the deck, allowing people to move around the ship in safety and clear of the incoming waves over the main upper deck. But for some reason, this young man who was taking some food to the galley to be cooked took a short cut along the main deck. He was not missed until it was reported that there was no food for that mess. When calmer weather returned, they found a sea boot with his name in it, jammed behind a heavy sea locker on the upper deck, and the lid of the locker was bent right back. It was assumed that he would have been dead before he was washed over the side.

The sea has awesome powers, and it makes you wonder how the ships can withstand the pounding they get. As long as they remain like corks, it's possible to weather the storms. Get water inside and as they say 'your sunk'. Our ship 'Armada' was rising and falling about twenty to thirty feet over the waves. One minute as the ship rose, you were struggling up hill, and you could feel your brain

40

The Armada Gang

in your skull being compressed, and your body seemed to weigh twice its normal weight. Next, as the ship dipped down into the trough of the wave, your body would feel light as if you were walking on air, and your brain was compressed in the other direction. The preparation of food became impossible, but the ship's chefs came to the rescue by managing to make up and cook large batches of soup. This was dished up to the messes in big pots that were strung up, by means of rope to the hammock bars, to stop the possibility of it sliding about. You would then scoop out a cupful and with one hand, holding on to something while you drank it.

When we finally cleared the storm, and reached calmer waters, we could assess the amount of damage. It amounted to the loss of nearly all the boats, for they had been smashed as they hung onto the davits. A lot of the guard rails had been bent right back. The old ship looked a poor sight, not now the smart paintwork and the painted green non-slip walkways, or even the steel chequered plate dressing blackleaded until it shone. But we took heart that this had happened a thousand times before with all navy ships. But there, we were going to put her into mothballs so it didn't really matter.

After the minesweepers were delivered to Southampton water, we carried on to Chatham, and once there, we had to remove all stores, ammunition, and everything not fixed down. This was to allow the dockyard to cocoon the whole of the upper part in a fibre-glass seal. This took some weeks to do. During that time I saw an Admiralty Fleet Order on the notice board. The 'A.F.O.' declared that volunteers were required for the Royal Yacht Britannia, soon to be brought into service. I was quite excited at the thought of a job like that, and I put in my request right away. Permission to see the Captain, through the First Lieutenant, through the Divisional Officer, to be considered for 'A.F.O.' That's how it had to be worded. When the other lads heard that I was going to volunteer, they all fell about laughing, there wasn't a snowball's chance in hell, as far as they were concerned. Once the request was completed and duly forwarded I carried on my duties and forgot about the request.

Once the ship had been cleared, it was towed off to be put into mothballs. The strange thing was, that we were all sad to see her go. Everyone became attached, for we had good times and bad times. Forgotten were the cockroaches that you seemed to find in every nook and cranny, the leaky turrets etc., etc. I am glad to say though that some years later she was brought out of mothballs, restored to good health, and went on to serve in the Home Fleet until 1965. As for her crew; we were all drafted back into Chatham Barracks, where we languished until the following February owing to the fact that our new ship had yet to be completed. Apart from a short gunnery course relating to the new type of armaments to be used on the new ship I managed to get a lot of home leave in. During that time I started seeing Pat Callow again. Quite casually at first and gradually more and more until we became an item.

There was a bit of consternation at first from the families as Pat was still an item with Ernie, who was in the Far East, but things worked out in the end, and when he returned, we both went to see him to resolve the situation. At the time of putting this down on paper, Pat and I have been married for fifty years. Our standing joke is I'll say 'it only seems like our wedding was yesterday' and she replies 'if it was tomorrow I'd cancel it'! Well I hope she is joking!

The time spent in barracks was divided by a gunnery course that was carried out at Whale Island, Portsmouth, a man-made island. This was the biggest gunnery school in England. This came about when the French prisoners of war, during the Napoleonic wars, were made to dig out the earth to build the dry docks in Portsmouth dockyard. This earth was then transported and dumped at a pre-arranged place. There was so much of it that an island was formed. I must say the place was put to very good use over the years. Although it was a bit old fashioned when I was there, it has now developed into a Guided Weapons School. Besides the schooling, I spent more time in the barrack guard, and the barrack fire brigade. This required constant practice with getting the water pumps to the imaginary fire, and the rescue ladder that had to be wound up to its full height by hand. I can tell you at times it was quite a sight to behold. During my time with the guard I was sent to London with the R.N. ambulance as a back up to the crew. Our destination was Millbank Hospital where a naval rating had been admitted. We had to bring him back to Chatham. Once he was safely installed in the ambulance, and me to keep him company, he told me that for some reason he had gone berserk and attacked people on the station. I could only hope it was because the train might have been late. All was well though, and we made it back to Chatham without him throwing any more tantrums.

The biggest surprise of all came when I was summoned to appear before a selection board. This was the result of my request for the Royal Yacht. The selection board was made up of naval officers, including an Admiral. They were interested in what sports I liked, interests, general intelligence etc, etc. I found out later that the police had enquired at my Dad's workplace about my past history.

I would be lying, if I said that I wasn't highly delighted at the turn of events that told me that I was at least being considered. At the same time I was surprised, for back in 1950 while on leave from H.M.S. Swiftsure, in company of my 'oppo' Stanley Dietman, we managed to get into a bit of bother with some young Royal Air Force chaps. I cannot remember what it was about now but a couple of deck chairs were broken. I have no idea who called the police, but when they arrived, Stanley and I were the only two on the scene. We tried to leg it, and were chased around Victoria Fountain outside Buckingham Palace by the police about three times, until they decided to just stand still and we came running around and into their arms! We were naturally arrested, and charged with malicious damage. We had to appear in court a few days later. Stanley and I did not dare tell our parents for fear of worrying them.

When we arrived at court we were surprised to see a naval officer waiting for us as our councillor. The judge listened to the police account and asked us what we thought we were doing that night and Stanley told him we were only having a 'skylark'. This was immediately seized upon by the local reporter who titled his article: 'Two Sailors on the Skylark'. As we had not told our parents anything about our predicament my Dad wasn't very pleased when one of his workmates pointed it out to him in the paper a couple of days later.

The officer asked for leniency, as we were liable to naval discipline when we returned to our ship. Seeing how the fracas started in Green Park and finished outside Buckingham Palace we were bound to cop it. And we did. Charged with disgracing the King's uniform, contrary to King's Rules and Regulations. This brought a term of eleven days stoppage of pay and leave. And eleven nights of all the rotten jobs they could find for us to do. So you see, I was quite surprised that I even made it to the first interview for the Royal Yacht Service. But once the interview was done I put it out of my mind, for I was told there were at least three thousand volunteers hoping to get picked.

The time passed and eventually our new ship was ready. The ex 'Armada's' crew was drafted, en masse up to Glasgow to embark on H.M.S. Delight.

Our new ship was just that, brand new. She was a Daring Class destroyer, the very latest design in fighting ships. It was going to be quite a task in getting to know her. I was partially clued up as we had been away to Whale Island for a revision on her armament. It was the 6th October 1953 now, and we had a schedule of four weeks to take the ship to sea for the working-up period, and after that we were to sail from the usual venue, Portland Bill, to take up our remaining year of commission in Malta.

I must admit that I was not too happy about going, as by now things seemed to be serious between Pat and I. For all that, the day arrived and after all the goodbyes had been said, we sailed for Portland. We spent the last part of the week at a buoy in the harbour. I was in the bathroom on Saturday morning, when the Coxswain, Chief Petty Office Regulator poked his head in and said; 'Saxby get your kit packed, you've got a draft to the Royal Yacht'. I was a bit shocked, and said 'You're joking'. To which he replied 'Saxby I never joke with you'.

The Coxswain and I never saw eye to eye when we were aboard the 'Armada'. This certain dislike had occurred during our time in Malta. The Coxswain had an office on the upper deck, just aft of the main superstructure. He would do the ship's organizing from there during the day but he used it like his own personal cabin where he would have his bed on the desk. He claimed that in doing this, you would always know where to find him. Most people thought he was a bombastic person who liked to live above his station.

What transpired was that when we were on a 'showing the flag' visit to San Remo in Italy, some lads returned from shore leave having consumed a great deal of Vino. Very merry for having done so, thought it would be fun to put a sea hose into the door of the Coxswain's office. Having put the dog clips on so that the door would hold the end of the hose from jumping about, turned the hose on and disappeared. I am sure the 'Cox' thought the ship was sinking. I don't know why, but he always thought that I had something to do with that little skylark, hence the ill-will that developed between us, and I am sure he would eventually wreak his revenge, so it was just as well I was leaving. I didn't blame him really, for having been woken up from his slumbers that way was awful.

It did not take long for the buzz to go around the ship that I had been given a draft chit to the Royal Yacht Britannia. My shipmates were happy for me, and a little incredulous that I had actually succeeded in my application. They were not the only ones, as I was a bit stunned myself. I was immediately invited around for sippers of everyone's tot.

Now the rum ration in the navy is, or was, a mysterious tradition. It stemmed from the times

The rum ration

when water was difficult to keep on board a ship. But wines and spirits were not, and that's what the crew received instead. The promise of free barrels of rum forever from the West Indies pinned the choice of a daily ration in the navy down to rum! In those days, the navy had young lads of twelve or so on board, but they were not allowed strong drink until they were fourteen. On their qualifying birthday, they apparently finished up drunk. The penalty for being drunk was a flogging! So you see the rum ration was a tradition that was steeped in history. Junior rating's tots were mixed with water, while Petty Officers' and Chief Petty Officers' was issued neat. Once water is added, the rum will not keep. But the senior ratings were trusted, and could save their ration in a bottle if they so wished.

It was used like money, if someone had done you a favour they would be invited around at the next tot time for 'sippers' if it was a small favour; 'gulpers' for a larger one and 'sandy bottom' for outstanding ones. In this atmosphere of celebration I was invited by all and sundry on Saturday tot time for 'sippers'. I managed quite a few messes and P.O's messes, but had to stagger back to my own mess, where I collapsed in a big heap. The lads put me on to one of the bunks right alongside a porthole. All I can remember of that Saturday and the most of Sunday was my continual heaving out of that port-hole. When I did finally regain my stature, I was surprised that the lads had removed my false tooth to stop me losing it. 'Good lads'. Not only that, but they had packed all my kit ready for me to go on draft the next day. What does that tell you about friends?

I left the ship next morning Monday 22nd November 1953. Just as she was getting ready to slip her moorings and start the passage to Malta. I watched as she left. Then I was promptly whipped away to the railway station at Weymouth, to make my return to Chatham.

Royal Yacht Service

On the train from Weymouth to London, where I had to catch a different connection for Chatham, I hatched a plan to break my journey to see Pat, who was employed at a couturier called Simmones in Curzon Street. Now as far as she was concerned I was on my way to Malta for I really had no time to let anybody know my good fortune. You can imagine the shock at seeing me turning up at her place of employment in the afternoon. She was convinced that I had deserted, but finally accepted my explanation. It was a bit risky doing what I had done, seeing there was quite a lot at risk. Nevertheless it was a risk worth taking, and all worked out beautifully, and afterwards, I continued my journey to Chatham, and did the usual joining routine. Mum and Dad were well pleased with the event as well as other members of my family.

The very next day; the 23rd November 1953, I was told to muster outside the drafting office, where to my surprise I was joined by five other ratings, who turned out to be like me, destined for the Royal Yacht. We were informed that we were to be the advance party, to travel the next day to John Brown's at Clyde Bank, Glasgow. Is that the place I had been to just recently? Of course it was, when we had to crew the H.M.S. Delight from the very same place. For the life of me, I cannot imagine how I never saw the Royal Yacht being built there on that occasion. The reason for the advance party was to set up some sort of security for the yacht in its final stages of completion. Things had happened so quickly that I must say we were in a little bit of a quandary. Who was who in our little group? We were all dressed the same, our Burberry raincoats over our uniforms, and that covered our badges of rank, so no one knew who was a Gunnery Rating, Leading Hand, or any other rate. Quite innocently I said I suppose we will get some bloody Petty Officer in charge of us when we get up there. Almost immediately, one of the lads took off his Burberry, revealing his crossed anchors denoting the fact he was a Petty Officer. 'No lads', he said 'you have got a bloody Petty Officer right now'. The reason we did not know his rank was due to the fact that he had recently been promoted, and had to serve a probationary period before he received his P.O.'s uniform of jacket and trousers, and peaked cap.

He turned out to be P.O. Dobson, 'Dobbo', as he was known after that. He became a lifelong friend, and a person I was very glad to have known. After all the necessary arrangements had been made, kit packed and assembled we were off to London to catch a train for Glasgow. This time we travelled in R.N. transport up to Euston station to catch a train in the late evening.

I seemed to live my life on trains since I joined the navy! Train stories come flooding back to me having said that, funny things that happened when travelling home to London from Chatham. Usually when the train pulled into London Bridge, all the matelots would leap out of the doors and career headlong down the platform. This particular time I was in the lead, and had not seen they were unloading the mailvan by throwing the bags out of the van and onto the platform. As I dashed by, one of these bags wrapped itself around my neck, carrying me onto the pile of bags on the platform. This raised a cheer from the passing matelots in full flight.

Another time one poor soul was trying to get on a train that was leaving, he managed to get the door open, and threw his little weekend case into the compartment. The lads inside must have been sure he would not make it, threw his case out again just as he managed to get a foothold and clambered in!

Sometimes we found it was quicker to disembark the train at Gravesend, catch the ferry from there to Tilbury and then have a shorter journey the rest of the way to London. On this occasion in the mad rush to get on the ferry, one lad in the front, saw the ferry about eight or nine feet away from the jetty so he took a flying leap over the water, desperate in the thought that he was about to miss the boat, then to the hilarity of the rest of us, realised that it was just coming in!

Back to the plot. When our transport arrived at Euston, Pat was there for the purpose of seeing me off. This had been arranged by us over the 'phone earlier in the day. It was more of a good luck gesture, than anything else, for it was not foreseen that we would be apart for long. The lads gave her a good cheer anyway as we kissed goodbye.

The twelve hour journey seemed interminably long, but we eventually arrived at the lower-level of Glasgow station. The whole area seemed to be covered in steam as we staggered out along the platform to collect our kit. It was quite a considerable time before we were collected by the R.N. and trundled off to John Brown's shipyard. This shipyard had a long and honourable history of building some of the most famous ships ever.

We were taken not to the ship, but to the dockyard office, where a gentleman told us that our billet was to be the sail loft in the dockyard. On our arrival at the sail loft we could not believe that better arrangements had not been made. Imagine our surprise to find that another rating A.B. Dennis Ivory ex-South African Navy, had already been living there for the week before we arrived. Not only that, but the navy had made no provisions for our pay. Dennis was to be part of the crew, but had leave owing to him so our arrival allowed him to hand over the fort to us, while he took off.

After a night's kip in the sail loft, a young sublieutenant turned up to take us on an introductory tour of the yacht. I turned the last corner and caught sight for the first time of 'Britannia'. It took my breath away. She was beautiful, with her bottle blue shining hull, and gleaming white superstructure it was more impressive than I could have ever imagined. The ship was finished except for internal work on the Royal Apartments.

Our inboard tour revealed that there was a very large, fully equipped laundry, an impressive sick bay and operating theatre. In fact the whole ship was designed to meet practically every emergency. That was readily understood seeing the sole purpose was to look after the Queen and all the Royal Family.

It was surprising to find out that the yacht was not launched until 16th April 1953 and was due to sail for our first royal duty on the 14th April 1954. I hasten to add that I did not know that date at the time. On reflection one can see there was not a lot of time between the two dates to assemble the crew, work the ship up into readiness, all to be done in four months. That explained the swiftness of mine and the others draft chits, to be at John Brown's on the 24th November 1953. After our tour, 'Dobbo' explained to the young sublieutenant that we had not been paid, and we could not afford to avail ourselves of lodgings. Sublieutenant Parry said he would see what he could do for us. He kept his word and returned with cash, drawn from his own bank account.

I met him many years after he had served on the yacht and then gone back to general service. We met at Highgrove House, having been invited to a garden party, in honour of ex-yachtsmen. By now he was a retired naval officer. I reminded him about the money, and said that I could not remember if we paid him back. He said 'If that's the case, then you are most welcome to it my boy'. He had a tie on covered with an elephant motif, and all their trunks had a knot in them. When I asked him to explain, he told me 'It is to remind me that I cannot remember a damn thing! Prince Charles was our host at the party, and when in the course of circulating, he came up to our little group, I related the story to him, which caused much amusement.

The money we received, although welcome, was still not enough to see us into lodgings. 'Dobbo' made the decision that we were going to move on board the yacht! We each picked out a nice little cabin. These cabins would later be for the Chief Petty Officers. We thought we might as well have

49

a bit of comfort, even if it was for the first and last time. After settling in we made the chief's pantry our kitchen with with cups, plates etc, and an electric kettle. Now we were set, for there was a fish and chip shop not far away. Also just across the road to the shipyard was a cafe. The cafe was one of the old versions, not all that clean, and purely functional. As you went in you had to bob down to get below the cloud of steam and tobacco smoke to see where you could sit, but this didn't put a hungry matelot off his food. Not far from the cafe, was a pub, I think we used it once. I don't think we were very welcome there for as we stood there having a drink, one of the shipyard workers spilt a drop of his beer down the front of me. I moved away and he followed me and repeated his 'little accident'. That was enough for us, as we intended to stay away from trouble. What the problem was with them mystified us and we did not intend to find out.

The reason that we were here was to effect some kind of security. It wasn't quite clear to us what exactly we were required to do, except to check passes that had been issued to all concerned with the building of the yacht. If you ever have the dubious pleasure of asking a Glasgow shipyard worker for his pass, especially one that has been working on the ship for the last couple of years, then you would have seen the look of disbelief in his eyes, and the only too explicit profanity as he swept by you.

But we did our best, and kept our sense of proportion and managed to get by without being thrown into the harbour. Our little group progressed throughout December this way, and was lucky enough for a couple of us to be able to go home on Christmas leave with the financial help from those remaining. I myself managed to drum up enough for my fare home, with just a little left to purchase my fare on the tube for the remainder of the journey. It was essential that we returned the day after Boxing Day. That I did, for the ship was to take her sea trials shortly after that. These sea trials were to be carried out by John Brown's, accompanied by naval staff to test every aspect of the ship's capabilities prior to accepting her. We had to go along too and help out. One of the tests was to be trials on the stabilisers, these were wings; very much like aeroplane wings. They were about nine feet long, and they could be retracted inside the ship, or put out either side. They were hydraulically operated, and the purpose for them was to stop the ship rolling too much. They could when worked by hand, make the ship roll. The object of the test was to get the stabilisers to produce a very big roll, then switch them to stabilise to see if they worked correctly, and how quickly they were effective. The first thing we had to do was lash down all moveable objects.

The trials were very good, and we managed to produce a forty degree roll. The humorous part was when we passed through the local fishing fleet doing a forty degree roll on a dead flat calm sea! I often wonder what those fishermen thought.

New Year came around, and we were invited to a party by one of our shipyard associates. He lived in the Gorbals, an area of Glasgow which in those days was a very run down and violent place to live, or indeed, visit. I was told that taxi drivers refused to enter the area. They would drop their fare on the outskirts for fear of the taxi being attacked! We still didn't have much money so we went by tram. Trams had long ago been scrapped in London. They ran on rails set into the road, and they made one hell of a row as they trundled along. The trams had a position for the driver at each end, and the backs of the seats, would fold so you could determine whether you sat with your back to the driver or not. This, as far as I can remember is the very last time that I ever rode on a tram.

We located his house, and indeed the whole place looked like a disaster area, with large wooden props on quite a few houses, apparently to stop them falling down. Once inside, his house was warm, bright and full of friendly people. Apart from the drinking, we had to do ritual things like going outside then coming back in again, only this time with a piece of coal that you had to give to the occupants. It was a good party judging by the hangover we had the next morning. Our host made it clear to us that it would not be safe to make our own way back to the tram so he escorted us to make sure, because he knew the ropes. Sure enough, on the way we were approached by a group of ghastly looking guys holding bottles containing what looked like methylated spirits. They offered us a drink from them, and when we refused they got angry, and reversed their hands on their bottles so they were now holding them like clubs. Seeing this our host called out for us to leg it and this we did rather smartly!

On the 8th January 1954, the main body of the ship's company arrived to embark. It was a great day for us all, but we knew that there was a lot of hard work to be done to make her fit for a Queen. After the ship's company had settled into their various accommodation we were off to sea for more trials. These would be the final ones before the navy accepted her. Unfortunately we encountered some very heavy weather during those trials which was seen as a good test for her seaworthiness. After that we sailed for Portsmouth. Once there the ship was swamped by carpenters, painters, and all sorts of technicians, for there was a lot of finishing work to be done in the Royal Apartments. In the meantime we were still learning how to run the ship, also getting measured for our new posh uniforms. These consisted of a doeskin jacket and trousers. The trousers worn outside the jacket, and secured by a silk bow at the back. Originally, there were shoes with the same sort of bow, instead of laces.

We had a big surprise the first time we turned up at Portsmouth station ready to go home on two weeks leave. The 'crushers' on duty there had never seen this outfit before, and promptly sent us back to the yacht for being 'out of the dress of the day'. It took a few phone calls to clear the way for us to carry on with our leave.

I have to admit, that I was very proud of myself dressed in my new outfit on my journey home. From my cap with its band inscribed Royal Yacht in gold letters, interspaced with a gold crown separating the two words, to my new suit with its gold badges of rank, and a Royal Yacht flash on the right shoulder. Gone the days of being a 'tiddly' sailor, I was now a befitting member of royal service. I must also admit that my ego was lifted when I could not help noticing people nudging one another when they noticed me and would bring it to the attention of whoever they were with.

The two weeks leave was spent wallowing in the well wishes of friends and relations. On one occasion while waiting outside Pat's place of work, a very well spoken gentleman came up and said 'Absolutely splendid my boy, good luck to you.' So it was that I had been catapulted into a different world, and one that I liked very much. After the leave period we were thrown back into learning how to run a royal ship. Some of the staff of the previous royal yacht 'Victoria & Albert', had also joined 'Britannia' but it was obvious from the start that they would not cope, seeing they were nearing the end of their service. They were of great help in giving us newcomers a jump start, in learning how to carry out our tasks by hand signals alone. No spoken words uttered for the purpose of silence when the Royal Family were on board. White deck shoes were provided for the same reason.

The date set for our departure from England was the 14th April 1954 our destination was firstly Malta and then Tobruk to meet Her Majesty the Queen and Prince Philip on their return from their world cruise, in celebration of her accession to the throne. The Royal children were embarked for the outward journey. They had to be guarded all the time, for it would not do to have one of them disappearing over the ship's side! I am glad to say the voyage out was extremely good, no rough weather at all.

One afternoon Prince Charles was brought down to the seamans mess deck to have tea with the sailors. This was done without any prior warning. This meant he sees at least a couple of ratings in their hammocks, for if you kept the middle watch the night before, midnight until 4am, then you were entitled to the afternoon off to catch up on your sleep. Prince Charles arrived with his minder, minus Princess Anne, it would not be fitting for her to be in the sailors mess! Bearing in mind that he was only six years old at this time, we sat him down at our table with a cup of tea and some bread and he quite

The Royal children arriving to start the journey to rejoin Her Majesty the Queen
and Prince Philip on the new yacht 'Britannia' ...
...and below I am on the left as one of the barges crew

H.M. the Queen and Prince Philip on the 'Britannia' for the first time

enjoyed himself, it was then that some bright spark told him it would be a good idea if he gave the sailor in his hammock a shake, and tell him it was time for tea. The sailor in question was a character by the name of Frank Boothman, 'Yorky Boothman'. Prince Charles did as he was asked, and Yorky peeped over the side of his hammock, and saw who was waking him up, reflected for a moment, then said 'Charles if you ever want to grow up to be King, then never shake a sailor in his hammock on his afternoon off!' It was a real heart stopper, we just could not believe he said it. Everything seemed to be alright though, for over the years Prince Charles has never mentioned it on the occasions we have had the privilege of being in his company from time to time.

This incident left us all a bit nervous, for we were all on a

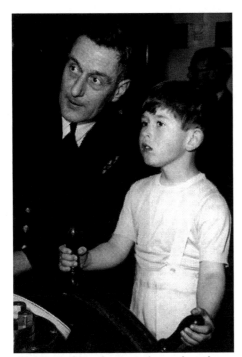
Prince Charles at the wheel....

year's probationary period. At the end of which the navy was to choose ninety ratings, out of the yacht's two hundred and fifty complement to remain as permanent royal yachtsmen. The remainder to be changed every two years, to give everyone in the navy a chance to serve on board her. As a result of this, one of my 'oppos' 'Joe Croft' served a total of thirty years, rising to the rank of Petty Officer.

In the end I was lucky enough to be selected, although I don't know how, to serve nearly nine years aboard her, until my service expired and I left the navy for 'civvy street'. On reflection, and often reminded by Pat it would have been better if I had signed on again like Joe.

....Princess Anne too

Back to the Royal children and this first trip. I was involved in another, embarrassing situation some time later. It occurred when A.B. Clench, 'Tubby' and I were detailed to be hoisted up to the top of the

mainmast to wash it. The mast had been made very grubby by an unfortunate blast of black smoke from the funnel. Bearing in mind the mast was seventy two feet high, it was quite a nerve racking business. Our ascent to the top of the mast was to be in 'bosun's chairs', these being small planks of wood, fitted with ropes. Once seated in them, you were hoisted up to the top by three strong
attendants. Then with our buckets of soapy water we started at the top and were lowered by our attendants.

Sometimes as a 'good for a laugh' joke, they let us go

down too quickly, and stopped us with a jerk. This worried 'Tubby' a great deal, and he let his feelings be known in a stream of foul language. Unknown to us, the Royal children were playing on the sun deck, just out of sight, but not out of hearing. Miss Peebles the children's governess, complained to the Admiral, so later on our party was reprimanded severely for inadvertently teaching the children new words!

We arrived at Malta on the 22nd April 1954 and were to remain for a week to spruce the yacht up for our momentous occasion of meeting Her Majesty in Tobruk on the 1st May 1954 on return from her world tour, travelling on board the R.M.S. Gothic. Unfortunately the yacht had not been ready in time for that part of the tour, so 'Gothic' was commissioned to have the honour. It promised to be quite dramatic, as the two ships were to meet at Tobruk where Her Majesty would transfer to her brand new Royal Yacht, Britannia.

My job at this particular time was as crew member on the royal barge. This was the Royal Family's transport to and from the yacht. It was a fantastic craft, decorated in blue, with maroon canopies, and gold fittings. The crew consisted of coxswain, 'driver', an officer, one stoker mechanic, and two seamen, one on the bow, and one on the stern. We really did look a splendid sight. All the crew immaculately dressed, both seamen holding boathooks, long varnished poles with hooks on the end. We would stand, one on the bow, and one on the stern, with our boathooks held vertically in front of us. Then at a signal from the bow man, in the form of a wiggle of his right elbow, he would tap his boathook twice on the deck, and in unison we would lift the hooks to a horizontal position above our heads, then in unison drop them to waist height ready to grapple whatever we were coming alongside. After a while we were very efficient at this boat drill, so it all looked quite spectacular.

Our First Royal Duty - The Queen

We arrived at Tobruk on the appointed date 1st April 1954 after leaving Malta to await 'Gothic'. It seemed very strange to me, for it was not a million years ago that I was in a landing party looking to face the Egyptian defence force, that luckily never appeared, in this very same place in Tobruk. Now 1 was in a different situation, a world away from a life of confrontation, to one of great esteem.

Everything went according to plan, Her Majesty transferred to 'Britannia' by the barge that had been used on the 'Gothic', and we set sail for Malta. On the return journey we were met by the Mediterranean Fleet. My old ship 'Delight' being one of them. Lord Mountbatten was transferred from the flagship to 'Britannia' to greet the Queen, and also to display our ability in transferring a person at sea.

The entry to Grand Harbour in Malta was to say in the least fantastic. This was a first time for us novices in royal protocol. We were not prepared for the thousands of people, waving and cheering, it really made the hair on the back of my neck stand up. I could not be more proud of being British. The Royal party had many appointments, and it now became the duty of the Royal Barge to transport them. My position on the barge was at the stern, which meant that this was the position that one had to get on or off. On one return journey, while Her Majesty was waiting to embark, and only being five feet away from me, I must admit my attention was distracted by looking at her instead of making sure that the barge was up close to the gangway. It was only when I noticed Prince Philip giving me a stare then dropping his eyes to the gangway then back to me again, that I realised that there was a gap of about a foot between the barge and the gangway. Her Majesty was waiting for me to close it, which I did rather smartly, she then stepped aboard. I don't think H.R.H. ever complained about the incident, for it was never mentioned. I suppose he realised that I was a little overawed by the new experience. In fact, I consider it as a little secret between him and me.

After a four day stay in Malta, we departed with the now complete Royal Family, being treated to an exciting farewell from the crowds, matching the enthusiasm that they were greeted with on their arrival. This then was the first leg of our voyage back to England, with one pre-arranged stop of two days with a royal visit to Gibraltar. It's strange how these different places; Malta, Gibraltar, Tobruk kept

SURNAME *SAXBY*

CHRISTIAN NAME *Charles*

This is to certify that the above-named is a British Subject.

Colonial Secretary.

My visa for Tangiers

emerging in my life. Gibraltar has special memories for me, seeing that I spent a fair amount of time there.

On one occasion while serving on board 'Armada', we had a rather long stay for a refit that had to be done in one of the dry docks there. It was to be quite novel for us because we had to live in accommodation huts alongside the dry dock while the repairs were done, and for the first time we were allowed to go ashore in civilian clothes! Not only that, we were going to be allowed four days leave if so desired. There was information giving us guidance on where to spend our welcome break from navy routines. My choice was a hotel that gave special rates to the members of British armed forces. The hotel was in Tangiers, and we needed visas from the Moroccan government.

Tangiers was about seven miles across the Straits of Gibraltar, a journey that took two hours by ferryboat. Once there, you stepped off the boat, and it seemed that you had stepped back in time for hundreds of years, for everything looked the same as it would have done in the time of Jesus. The narrow streets and their bazaars, the Arabs sipping their mint tea, donkeys, beggar children, and the Casbah, a place that had a multitude of sins.

Our hotel turned out to be extremely nice, westernised but with Moroccan style and staff. In fact it was the first hotel I had ever been in! There were eight of us staying there, soldiers and air force, all lumped together in two big rooms. At mealtimes we would drive the waiters mad by demanding 'Ali, more bread!'. Poor old Ali would look out of the kitchen, and repeat incredulously, 'more bread?'.

The second night we were there we were advised to stay away from the town centre that night, for a troopship carrying French Foreign Legionnaires was at the docks taking on supplies. So the town that night was not a healthy place to be. We did not need telling twice, as we were here for a holiday, not as hospital fodder! I thoroughly enjoyed my visit to the old world, and all too soon had to return to reality, and was sad to hear that the group that chose to go for their break, over the border to La Linea, in Spain had been robbed on the first night at their hotel, and had to return right away. I was pleased I had chosen Tangiers.

The voyage to Gibraltar was calm and uneventful, apart from the unfamiliar sight of the warships that escorted us. The whole crew had now slipped into their daily routines of official royal duties. My own duties along with the rest of the quarterdeck part of ship, was to clean the upper deck part of the Royal Apartments. This would involve turning up to work at 7am, cleaning all the brass fittings, washing down paintwork, and scrubbing the decks with silent electric deck scrubbers. All this had to be done by 8am, in complete silence, no spoken orders, all hand signals by the Petty Officer. This would leave that part of the yacht clean and free for the family to use as they wished, no one was allowed there after 8am, except for vital necessities.

The reception at Gibraltar was even more lively, as we were now in an even more British colony, I hoped it would remain so for a long time in the future. I think that all these boisterous greetings were preparing us, the crew, for the eventual one on the final return to England. This was apparently organised as a triumphal progress up the River Thames, and into the heart of London.

During the time before our intended return, the crew members were offered the opportunity of obtaining passes for their families for a good viewing point on Hay's Wharf in London Docks. I think there must have been limited numbers, for only my sister Alice and my Mum went there while Pat, managed to get a position on the big day on Butler's wharf. For the life of me, I cannot remember how it worked out that way.

The yacht arrived back in England on the 15th May 1954, pausing at the Isle of Wight for the Prime Minister, Sir Winston Churchill, to embark and accompany us on the journey up to London. It was a wonderful experience for everybody concerned, with the flags, the bands, and the thousands of cheering people.

Once the Royal Family had disembarked, the yacht was no longer on royal duty. This allowed us to let limited numbers of our families visit the yacht for a sightseeing tour. That royal duty done, there were many more to come, we returned to Portsmouth to take up our permanent berthing position at, wait for it, Whale Island, only to be tied up between two buoys so we would not swing about with the tides. The access to the ship was by a very long floating pontoon. That could be a very odd experience when using it if the water was a bit choppy.

This then was home for 'Britannia' when it was not on royal functions, for it was out of the way in a backwater of Portsmouth harbour. We still had the little sightseeing boats calling round, to allow the holidaymakers a look at us. There was one other momentous occasion while we were in London. Pat said 'yes' to my proposal asking her to marry me. This was not for the first time of asking, but this time she had made up her mind. We were married the following year in London on the 27th August 1955.

Our next duty was to be Cowes Week. This was a traditional visit to the Isle of Wight sailing regattas. Yachts from all over the world would come along to compete. The 'Britannia's' attendance adding a great deal of importance to the occasion. This was of course all new to us, and we felt quite proud when we were moored at Cowes and to have all these splendid boats fussing around us. Even more so when it was learned that Earl Mountbatten and his family were coming to stay on board for the week. That was in addition to the Royal Family, so it was going to be a busy week for us. I was still a member of the Royal Barge crew, and we were sent over to a small fishing village, Hamble in Southampton waters, to meet the Earl and his family who were driving down.

The barge arrived at Hamble and we secured alongside the jetty to await the arrival of the Mountbatten family. The barge's officer was a bit concerned that the car transporting them would have difficulty in locating the correct turning that would bring them to the jetty. He directed me to go up to the main street, and when the car approached, I was to salute, and at the same time point in the direction that the chauffeur should take. There was a very big crowd waiting to see them, I don't know how they found out that someone special was arriving. The car approached, I saluted and pointed. The chauffeur, nodded his understanding, duly turned right. I then trotted after the car when the car suddenly stopped. The Earl's head popped out of the window, and he said to me 'Are you from the barge?'. 'Yes sir' I answered. He threw open the door and said 'Well get in lad.' So I did, finishing up sitting with the Mountbatten family. When we arrived back at the jetty, the chauffeur opened the door, and I jumped out and went to make my way back to the barge. The Earl stopped me in my tracks when he called out 'Don't forget the luggage lad'. So in a short space of time, my ego was lifted, and then brought back to earth with a bump!

A couple of days later we were to see the other side of the Earl's temperament for it was necessary to transport him back to Hamble by barge, as he was to attend an important meeting as quickly as possible. Now the barge had three engines and with their combined power produced twenty-six knots, pretty fast. We had completed about a quarter of the trip, when one of the engines stopped. We were able to carry on with the other two, but at reduced speed. He was not very happy about this. Then the second engine stopped, and once again the speed was reduced to a tragic eight knots. He was fuming, for it was going to take ages to reach Hamble, and it did. It was discovered later that water had found its way into the fuel. But for all that I was proud to have been not only in the company of this great man, but being part of the barge's crew, partially responsible for his safety. He was after all Governor of the Isle of Wight, Viceroy of India and an Earl, just to mention a few of the long list of titles. I was very sad when he was killed with his grandson, in a cowardly act by the I.R.A.

We finished off the first year, with a visit by H.R.H. Duke of Edinburgh to Canada, touching on Montreal, Quebec, Labrador and Goose Bay. After which we made the return journey for him to disembark at Aberdeen, 'the Granite City', this being the nearest point to his real destination of Balmoral, to join the Royal Family on their annual Scottish vacation.

We remained there for a few days, during which time I was among a coach party of yacht's crew that had been invited to visit Balmoral. The ride through the spectacular scenery of the Deeside was a treat on its own. But Balmoral was something else, for you could feel the history that made up the place. We viewed the gardens, and were surprised to find out that the ice pits were still in use. These were brick built pits, that were filled with ice during the winter, that lasted all through the summer. All the food supplies were stored in there, and it was reached by a tunnel from inside the castle.

I was also impressed when I visited the garages, for there were fourteen cars in there, ranging from the Prince's Aston Martin to the Rolls Royce. As I chatted to one of the chauffeurs, who was busy polishing a Bentley, I leaned on the mud guard. His face turned red and he quickly pushed my hand off the car explaining that the heat of my hand would melt the build up of the wax coating, and would likely take him weeks to correct the mark it would leave. Trust me to upset the apple cart.

Aberdeen was the place where I saw, indeed, even heard of for the first time, Lonnie Donegan. My 'oppo' Ginger Gilbert, and I went to see 'out of curiosity' this skiffle group that was performing at a little jazz club in the town. We were so impressed by him that we decided on the spot to follow his example and form our own group on the yacht. It turned out to be a big success, with our tea chest double bass, washboard and thimbles, trumpet and last but not least, snare drum. There was a certain amount of bother when we tried to practice. A number of places were tried with the object of not annoying anybody. In the end we were consigned to the propeller shaft room. This was the chamber that the propeller shaft ran through, it was roomy enough but the rumble of the shaft going around driving the propeller was not the ideal accompaniment to our attempts at making music. As it was we had the honour of appearing in front of H.M. the Queen on at least four occasions, performing in the yacht's 'Sods Opera', that she always liked to see when on longer trips.

The 'Sods Operas', were always a great success with the Royal Family. The cast was made up from enthusiastic volunteers, who put many hours into rehearsals in their spare time. Some of the characters in the opera would not possibly be associated with their responsible jobs on the yacht, you just would not recognise them for who they really were.

Three of the operas were really well done, very ambitious. They were; 'Fountain Lake Follies', 'Cinders at Sea' and 'Drop of a Brick'. All of which were rehearsed and perfected, and performed to a test audience made up of our nearest and dearest families. Two were performed at the Victory Theatre in Victory Naval Barracks, and one on board the yacht. The idea was of course to give our families the thrill of seeing our efforts, and of course their opinions to shape any modifications that was needed to improve the end product, making them fair viewing for the Royal Family. The last of our royal duties had been performed for that year, and the plan was for us to stay at Portsmouth for some modifications to the Royal Apartments, to combat a mysterious drumming noise when at sea. This noise had caused some concern for H.M. We had travelled a total of 20,576 miles in this the first year. The following year was to be momentous, but we did not know that we were to make more history concerning royalty.

THE SHIP'S COMPANY OF

HER MAJESTY'S YACHT BRITANNIA
(By kind permission of Vice-Admiral Sir Conolly Abel Smith, K.C.V.O., C.B.)

PRESENT

AT THE
DROP OF A BRICK

A CHRISTMAS DECORATION

THE

VICTORY THEATRE

63

Some of the cast

C A S T

(In order of appearance - We Hope)

****

Officer of the Watch	Ldg/Wtr	Heighway
Commander	Chief M.(E)	Shaw
Coxswain	Mechanician	Gardner
Measdeck Petty Officer	Yeoman	Dellenty
Able Seaman Shirk	Ldg/Phot	Smith
Ldg/Seaman Shifty	Mr Crompton	Sn Cd Engr.
Able Seaman Shady	Signalman	Taylor
Able Seaman Kristy	A.B.	Clench
Ordinary Cinders	Ch Yeo/Sigs	Penson
P.M.O.	Ldg/Cook	Pickering
A.B. Curly	C.E.R.A.	Peter
Doctor Kinsey.	Ldg/Stwd	Britteon
The Admiral	Yeoman	Dellenty
Ldg/Wren Draftemall.	L.E.M.	WOODS
Patrolmen	Lieut (E)	Collins
	C.P.O.	Goddard
C.P.O. Justice	C.E.R.A.	Peter
C.P.O. Braken & 1st Lieut.	Sailmaker	Smith
Senior Engineer	Himself	

****

Dance Speciality Act:- A.B. Coxon, A.B. Saxby, L/Stwd Britteon
L/Cook Pickering, C.P.O. Goddard
C.P.O. Peter - trained by Miss
Hunters School of Close Harmony
and the Tunbridge Wells Corps-de
Ballet.

Red Gilbert Sextet:- Messrs, Saxby, Gilbert, Coxon,
Mesher & Pickering, conducted by
Maestro Westlake, straight from
their successful Carribean Tour.

The Boulders Sisters:- Discarded by The Luton Girls Choir.

Mouthorganists :- M.(E)'s Stabler & Thornberry.

Songs :- L.S.A. Windle - BRITANNIAS' only
Howling Success.

IF YOU WERE THE ONLY GIRL IN THE WORLD

If you were the only girl in the world
And I was the only boy,
Nothing else would matter in the world today
We could go on living in the same old way,
A Garden of Eden just made for two
With nothing to mar our joy,
There would be such wonderful things to do
I could say such wonderful things to you,
If you were the only girl in the world
And I was the only Boy.

****

APRIL SHOWERS

Though April Showers may come your way
They bring the flowers that bloom in May,
So if its raining have no regrets
Because its raining, rain you know
Its raining Violets,
And When you see clouds upon the Hills
You soon will see crowds of Daffodils,
So keep on looking for the Bluebird
And listening for his song,
Whenever April Showers come along.

****

YOU
   AIN'T
      FINISHED
         YET :-
            (JUST TURN ME OV

Our skiffle group

Princess Margaret

The second year began with the controversy over Princess Margaret. Apparently she had become attached to one of the aides at the palace. He was Group Captain Peter Townsend. Unfortunately for her, he was a divorcee. The strict rules of protocol of the Royals was that it was forbidden to marry such a person, as in the case of Edward VIII and Mrs Simpson in 1936. H.M. did not actually forbid Margaret marrying him, but gave her the choice of keeping her titles of H.R.H. or lose them if she became Mrs Townsend. She eventually chose to keep her titles.

It was decided by the Palace to send Margaret on an extended tour of the West Indies to help her regain her poise after the recent troubles she had been through. Although the news of the forthcoming trip was quite exciting to us, I don't think it was received in the same light by the families. Especially Pat, for this was to be our wedding year. She had decided to make her own wedding dress, as well as the bridesmaids dresses, for this was her trade. It would be a busy time for her, and I think she would have appreciated a bit more support at that time. With our long stay in Portsmouth, our seagoing abilities was a little jaded so we were sent off to do a working-up period of a week. After which we sailed for the West Indies on the 18th January 1955. There was one stop at the Azores which is practically mid Atlantic, then on to the island of Trinidad.

The Azores was a strange set of islands, which are not well known to our society and once colonised by the Portuguese. While there we took on a consignment of bread, which they apparently baked in the ground under hot stones. That was a quite novel thought to us, until we cut some slices, and to our horror, found bits of grit and cigarette ends neatly embedded in them!

Our arrival in Trinidad was timed to be a few days before H.R.H. arrived, to allow us to spruce up the yacht after the long voyage across the Atlantic. She would be flying out, I remember her arrival very well, for I was struck by her appearance, in a white polka dot dress and her jewellery creating a fabulous freshness.

Our berth in Trinidad was behind an arena that was hosting a calypso competition. Naturally the island was full of music as they take it very seriously indeed. It was not surprising then, that once the lads were ashore, fuelled up on the lovely inexpensive rum they could be found following the crowd

H.R.H. Princess Margaret boarding 'Britannia'

wiggling and dancing behind the large vehicles carrying the steel bands parading around the town.

I was still a member of the barges crew, and it fell on us to transport H.R.H. to and fro at the different islands. I don't think she was carrying out any Royal duties, it was her decision where she wanted to go. The local dignitaries would fall over themselves to entertain her. After all this was a cruise to let her recuperate. Being barges crew brought us into close contact with her, naturally being that close at hand allowed us to see, as the cruise progressed, that she was more than capable of recuperating!

The West Indies is a beautiful area, and I can see why it was chosen for this trip. The days passed in balmy conditions, with the daily routine of rising early to clean the royal upper decks until they shone in the brilliant sunshine. If the yacht was not moored at one of the big islands, it would be en route to another one. But if H.R.H. wanted to stop for a shoreside picnic, 'ban yan', then we would drop anchor and stay for a while, there did not seem to be any timetable to stick to, which made it quite leisurely up to a point for us.

One such island was Mustique. The island was apparently owned by her personal friend Colin Tennant, and we were to stay there for a day or two. Later on, Mustique was to play a very large part in some of her mistakes. Now

H.R.H. Princess Margaret

69

when she desired to go ashore there, we would take her in the Royal Barge; trailing a small dinghy behind us. This was because the beaches were so shallow you could not get in far enough to let her disembark. We would anchor off a little way, then use the dinghy to row her the remainder of the way in. These were great trips for us as we had to stay on the beach with the Royal Party, they on one end of the beach, us on the other. At Mustique we would be supplied with sandwiches and soft drinks by guys in red jackets and black bow ties, compliments of Colin Tennant. Our job was to hang about on the beach until she wanted to return on board, well someone had to do it!

Other days on different islands it would only be a 'ban yan', organised by the officers for her, but none the less quite pleasant. H.R.H. arranged for her own hairdresser to be on board with her for the whole trip. That meant they were the only women on board. On one occasion when my 'oppo' Bert Cousins and I were mustered on the gangway ready for a trip ashore the officer of the watch, inspecting us to see that we were correctly attired, asked us if we would like to escort the hairdresser Sylvia as it would not be prudent for her to go ashore alone. It was a bit of a surprise to us both, but the novel idea appealed to us, and off we went. Our destination was the Pelican Bar that had found favour with the lads, and they had sort of adopted it as their own for the duration of the stay.

We received a few comments from the lads gathered there on seeing Sylvia in our company, but she mingled with them, and attracted the attention of one young A.B. seaman, by the name of Jephcott who took quite a shine to her. She also took a shine to him, this then was the beginning of a romance. He eventually wooed and finally won her during the remainder of the trip, they were married some time later, and spent a long life together running a hairdressers and a cafe, in Sandwich, Kent. We all met up a couple of years ago, and they were still very much together.

Sometimes when one was ashore, and H.R.H. passed by in an official car, she would see us in the crowd, and give us a friendly wave. This was an easy thing to happen, for the size of towns on the islands were usually quite small, and there was no mistaking our white tropical uniforms.

But then she wasn't always 'goody two shoes', for on a couple of occasions, the barge would arrive at a jetty to meet her on her return from some party or social gathering, only to find that instead of her turning up at the appointed time she would arrive hours later usually a bit tiddly. So much so that we would make sure that she managed to embark safely. H.R.H. did like her refreshments, and her cigarettes.

On one return trip, it was found that the ornate box that should have been full of her favourite cigarettes, was in fact empty. It was a case that someone had forgotten to fill it up, or someone had been smoking heavily. As it was, one of her aides turned to us at the stern of the barge and asked if anyone could supply any cigarettes. I had a packet of unopened Export Wild Woodbines in my pocket and I handed them over to him. H.R.H. took a cigarette from the packet, put it into her holder, lit and puffed away. That was the last I saw of my fags, so I always considered that she owed me twenty Woodbines! As long as she enjoyed them then of course she was quite welcome, I knew what it was like to want a puff. Fortunately I have long since given the habit up. On reflection, observing her demise, I think she would have been wise in those days to have given them up too.

The trip with Margaret was drawing to a close. We had visited: Trinidad, Tobago, Grenada, St. Vincent, Barbados, Antigua, St. Kitts, Mustique, Jamaica, Nassau, Bermuda, besides the other small islands for 'ban yans'. This was not the last time we were to visit the West Indies, far from it, as there was to be three more consequent Royal occasions that demanded our presence. As I said before someone had to do it!

After we left the West Indies, our next job was to be right over the other side of the world to receive the Duke of Edinburgh, on the 10th March at Villefranche in the Mediterranean, where he was to attend N.A.T.O. exercises. The yacht was to take part acting as one of a convoy with American submarines stalking us. That made us a bit nervous, for the Yanks are always a little bit over enthusiastic, and might get carried away and sink us! Only joking.

The passage over was uneventful except for when we stopped to box the compass. To do this it was necessary to lower a boat as a focal point, then the ship would steam around it at a fair distance and take compass bearings at different intervals to test the accuracy of the compass. Just one guess to who was in that boat! We were supplied with provisions and set adrift for four hours. The yacht was circling us for all that time, nearly out of sight on the horizon. I realised at that time what it must have been like to have had the awful experience of being adrift. Bobbing up and down in that small boat didn't do any favours to our stomachs, and we were very glad when the exercise ended.

After the N.A.T.O. exercises the rest of the year was taken up with our Cowes Week etc., with the exception of two occasions. One was the Fleet Review by H.M. the Queen. A proud moment, for the British Fleet was arranged in lines at Spithead, Isle of Wight. The Queen reviewed her Fleet from on board the yacht which steamed up and down the ranks of warships. She received three cheers from each one we passed. I still remember the prickly feeling up and down my spine, every time it happened.

The second occasion was a visit once again by H.M. the Queen to Douglas, Isle of Man. There is apparently a superstition that whenever the Monarch visits the island a mysterious fog would always descend and cover the place. We arrived on the 6th August and sure enough the legend lived up to its name by blotting out everything. As the visit was only a very short one I never managed to see the Isle of Man at all.

By now I had one thing on my mind, for I was to be married on the 27th August! The race was on to arrange everything by that date. Pat had finished the dresses, and she and I had booked a hall for the reception. It was actually the community centre in the middle of a block of flats, in Old Ford Road. It was practically brand new at that time, and the structure was 70% glass. It turned out to be a splendid and memorable venue for our reception. There was also the business of having the wedding banns read out three times at the church. During one of the readings, Pat and I were both startled by a very loud bang, it sounded like a gunshot in the silence of the church. The vicar apologised for making the noise, for he had slammed shut the book he was holding, saying 'I am sorry for the noise, and sorry for the little life I have just taken but these moths played havoc with the drapes in the church'!

I had not been idle in my time at Portsmouth, for I had found, and rented a little flat in St. Augustine Road in Southsea. Not much of a place to shout about but it would suffice to kick off our married life. I had by now served my one year's probationary period and I was one of the fortunate one's to have been chosen to stay on to be a permanent royal yachtsman. Which of course meant that I would stay on her for as long as I was serving in the Royal Navy. So you see we could make definite plans, without the danger of suddenly being sent off somewhere; a whole career was there if I so desired.

The great day arrived, 27th August 1955. The wedding was to take place at the Holy Trinity Church, Stepney. The best man was to be Pat's brother Eric. To support me in my hour of need, I had three 'oppos' from the yacht: Ginger Gilbert, Ron Westlake and John.

The programme for the occasion was the wedding ceremony, on to the reception after the photographs, then when the reception had finished at the 'Glass House' we would then move on to Pat's parents' house at 71 Ellesmere Road to continue through the rest of the night. Next day, Pat and I were to be taken by car to the station to catch our train to Portsmouth and take up residence in our rented flat.

The wedding went well, so many people! The reception was excellent and went off with a bang, except when I was lured away to look for a piano player, by Pat's Uncle Harry. This escapade took us to a local pub, where I think we stayed a bit too long. I was not very popular with Pat, but we were successful in securing a piano player to bash away the rest of the night.

At 11.30pm we had to vacate the Glass House. Everyone had a whale of a time during the evening, and were invited to continue at Pat's place. On hearing that, John one of my yachtie buddies, who had consumed quite a lot of drink yelled: Yippee! and immediately sank to the ground 'soused'! He was not seen again that night, and spent all that time on the bed in the back room at number 71.

The party continued until about 5am. I was told that neighbours two streets away were complaining! As things drew to a close, sleeping bodies occupied every spare bit of space in the house. Finding it impossible to get a bit of privacy for myself and Pat, we resorted to curling up in the back of her Dad's car outside the house!

Very early on Sunday morning, Pat and I were surprised to see John, our missing matelot coming down the front door steps, no shoes on, looking like death warmed up. He wanted to go and buy a newspaper, some milk and fags. As it was too early for shops to be open, we often wondered where he managed to get two bottles of milk and a newspaper that he had when he returned. My guess was that someone was short of those things on their doorstep that morning, he never did tell me.

Sunday afternoon was the planned time for my brother-in-law to drive Pat and I to the station, but fate took a hand once again, for my niece Carol suddenly developed stomach pains, so Charlie, her Dad took her to the hospital in the car. We waited for him to return to find out what was wrong with her, it turned out to be appendicitis.

At last we were on our way, and we finally arrived at our little flat. The journey down on the train was a strange one, with the realisation that we were an item now starting a whole new life together. The flat consisted of one bedroom upstairs and a living room and kitchen downstairs. The bed had wonky legs, that moved with a boing sound when you got into it. That took us by surprise on the first night, I can tell you. We settled down there but it wasn't long before we became dissatisfied, especially with the landlord's son. We called him the ginger headed monster, a nasty piece of work.

Our marriage was at the beginning of my two week annual summer leave, so we had plenty of time left to enjoy our honeymoon. The seaside was only a short walk from the flat, as was the Odeon cinema, and the Black & White Milk Bar, where we often used to have a cup of Horlicks on the way home!

It seems funny to call it a honeymoon, for when you equate it with the present day possibilities of expensive, and exotic honeymoons it wasn't even in that league. It was the best we could afford at the time, and it is quite obvious that the memories stay with us just as much.

After my leave finished and I had returned to duty, Pat found a job for herself, we began to look like an old married couple. The yacht had only one short trip that end of the year, so we had a nice quiet period to look forward to. The 'Britannia' had steamed 40,688 miles that year. Maybe I should not have said quiet as I had been talked into taking part in another of the 'Sods operas', that was to take place on one of the trips in the coming year. This meant a lot of rehearsals, songs to be learned, and dance routines to remember. Pat was of great assistance and she helped a lot, with her memory of lyrics, and by helping me to learn the scripts. I was also in the middle of doing a course to pass my test to become a Leading Seaman for more money. Pat would help out with this as well. I had fixed up a gadget, that was a battery and bulb, wired up to two dinner knives. When the knives were touched together the bulb would light up! Then we would sit in the darkened room, and she would send words to me in morse code, which I endeavoured to read. It usually ended up in an argument in who was right and who was wrong!

I eventually passed my test with a commendable 76.5 %, well that was good for me! Although I passed, it would be a long time before I would be made up to a Leading Seaman. This was because of the 'dead man's shoes' system that prevailed in the Royal Yacht Service. You have to wait until a Leading Seaman left before you could fill the vacated position.

The rest of the year was uneventful, with the exception of spending Christmas at home with our families.

My First Circumnavigation of the World

The New Year started as usual, with our work-up period, to get us to the efficiency required for our forthcoming period of royal duties, and to iron out any snags. We also had a lot of new members of crew joining us. I have already pointed out that in the system there were ninety permanent 'yachties,' the rest would would be swopped every two years, to give everyone in the navy a chance to serve on 'Britannia'. These new members had to be trained into the system. It was remarkable how quickly they performed. It was due to the fact that there was no strict discipline, everyone was put on trust to do their duties to their utmost, and it all worked very well.

The first duty of the year was to take H.R.H. Duke of Edinburgh, known to the Scots as 'Chookie Embra', on his involvement in the NATO exercises. I must admit that these exercises became a little boring. For they all proceeded at a slow pace, and it was always our job to be hunted.

The next part of the trip was a lot more interesting, for we were to visit Corsica and Sardinia. This was an official function by H.M. the Queen to Ajaccio in Corsica. This time the Royals included Princess Alexandria. A charming young lady, she would stop and chat to anyone. I nearly had the misfortune of headbutting her up the rear end while rushing up a ladder, not realising that she was just in front of me, after visiting the yacht's boiler room!

It turned out to be more like a pleasure cruise rather than a State Visit for we explored the coasts of Corsica and Sardinia stopping at various places. One such place was Valenco Gulf where we dropped anchor.

It was proposed that we had a large 'ban yan' on the beach and also decided was the rather dodgy untried manoeuvre of lashing two 'jollyboats' together; lowering the royal Land Rover enabling it to be put ashore. It all went very well.

As a footnote on the 'jollyboats', they were lovely 25ft open motor boats that had derived their name from their historic role in transporting sailors ashore to seek their pleasure - need I say more? Incidentally these two 'jollyboats' were sold at a later date during a period of upgrading the yacht for more practical means of water transport. Some twenty years later I found they were in the possession of a pleasure boat owner R.Tibbs Tonbridge Waterways Limited, on the river Medway, and he was

Corsica ban yan

running trips up and down the river, starting at Tonbridge Castle. Pat and I went down there to see for ourselves, and had a spin on the pristine looking 'jollyboat'. Sitting on there in the summer afternoon, with Pat and our dog Honey, seemed a remarkable turn of events that brought back floods of memories of bobbing about on the Atlantic for hours, while the yacht 'boxed the compass' around us. Or the time I joined in an expedition hoping to shoot a few crocodiles in Gambia, more about that later. Even to some of our icy trips to the English survey station in Antarctica, also more later. All nostalgic memories very much cherished.

The 'ban yan' exercise went well, the Land Rover was safely put ashore. We erected a huge tent made from a large tarpaulin. This was done by an overwhelming amount of willing helpers. A great bonfire was lit in front of the tent. Bangers and other goodies, 'beer' had been supplied. I am afraid H.M. the Queen never joined our party, but H.R.H. Princess Alexandria arrived and partook of a banger or two. The day ended when it snowed for the first time in twenty-five years in Corsica. The remaining part of the trip took us for further visits to Sardinia, then back home via Gibraltar.

The next time we left Portsmouth was in June for official attendance by H.R.H. Princess Margaret to Middlesborough and Oslo right after that. The time spent at Middlesborough gave rise to another story in the long line of funny happenings to me. The crew was invited to look around the steel works, having done so we were presented with a large nail that was produced there as a memento of our visit! During that evening I took myself off for a couple of beers. Nobody else seemed to be interested, as it was a drizzly night. The pub I eventually chose was right opposite the Town Hall. As soon as I walked in, I was greeted with a cheer as there were lads from the same steel works at the bar. I was invited to join them, and have a pint of Bass.

Unbeknown to me this was very strong beer, and it wasn't long before it had me under its influence. After a couple more, I realised that it would not be long before I would be unable to be in control. After saying my thanks and once outside I came to realise that I had drunk too much of the heavy Bass for it was very difficult for me to see the time on the Town Hall clock, and it was as large as Big Ben. I made my way to the local cinema, and bought a ticket, and after a little bit of difficulty, settled down on a seat in the comforting darkness. That was the last I remembered. I woke up about two hours later to find that there was a big empty space around me. There was dribble all down the front of my raincoat. I must have been making an awful snoring and snorting sound, that people were staying away from me. I had sobered up quite a lot, so I crept back on board while the going was good.

After the Oslo visit we were to do our usual Cowes week in July followed as usual by the Western Isles holiday for most of the Royal Family. The difference being, that we had been informed by no less than H.R.H. Prince Philip that at the end of August it was intended that the yacht was to do a world tour incorporating the Olympic Games that was going to take place in Melbourne, Australia. The 'Games' were going to be opened by himself, all this was going to take about seven months!

The laundry crew and myself keeping everyone clean during the trip

It was quite a shock, when during the Western Isles cruise H.R.H. gathered the ship's company on the upper deck to deliver the news of his forthcoming Geophysical Year Trip. This immediately posed a problem for me, as I could not leave Pat on her own in Southsea for that long. It was finally decided that she would return to London and live upstairs in my Mum's house 24 Gawber Street, until we returned. She did go back, and she managed to get her old job again. So I was happy that she was safe in an environment that she was used to.

While on the subject of jobs, I had been given a job change, for they had moved me into the laundry. It was a good move as far as I was concerned. For although they did not charge the crew very much for their finished laundry, whatever profit was made 10% of it was shared among the laundry crew! Extra dough, just what I needed. My 'oppo', P.O. Dobbo was in charge of the laundry, there was a good friendly bunch of guys already working in there, so we were in for an interesting seven months.

Life in the laundry was a complete revelation to me. It bore no resemblance to life on the upper deck as a seaman. For a start; there were two full crews, who each worked a twelve hour shift, and twelve hours off. That meant that we were all excused any watchkeeping or duties concerning running the ship. Our one and only job was the laundry. Our day would be to check in the new batch of washing, making sure all the items were marked with the individuals personal numbers. Once that was done the wash process would start. We were fully equipped with all sorts of steam presses for the different articles. Even to the very large one called a Callender for instantly drying and ironing sheets. There were small machines for processing the starched shirts and stiff collars as worn by the officers for dining and a steam press for the use on suits and woollen clothing.

The work would continue late into the evening until all had been washed, pressed, and partially racked up in the individual numbered compartments. Every thing was squared away ready for the opposite shift to start their twelve hour shift by beginning to mark in their day's laundry, by nine o'clock. We soon found out when on Royal duty that by making sure that the Royal galley 'kitchens', always had plenty of clean aprons, towels, and cloths in their ready to use wicker baskets then they would always return the compliment, by making sure that the early morning laundry crew had hot coffee and bacon rolls for breakfast in the laundry, such is life! Any surplus to requirements, ice cream etc, it was a case of you scratch my back etc. Working there was O.K. while we were in moderate climates, but once in the tropics, oh boy, the temperature rose to over 120 degrees Fahrenheit. I lost quite a lot of weight during that trip!

The process of stocking the ship with all the essential requirements for our voyage was a mammoth task. Everything from spares for the engineers, to a large amount of stores for the N.A.A.F.I. shop, fags and beer. The beer received special attention by being stored in one of the empty water tanks, so carefully packed from top to bottom, that when the last box was placed in the empty space, they were just able to close the hatch down! The N.A.A.F.I. shop was a boon on the yacht. A great gathering place that sold just about everything. It was managed by Dougie Jackson, and Brian Best. Both N.A.A.F.I. employees. Great characters.

So it was on the 28th August 1956 we left Portsmouth on the first leg of our voyage, bound for Mombasa via Sierra Leone, where we stopped for fuel. A short visit to Cape Town and Simon Town then on to Mombasa to prepare for the arrival of Princess Margaret for her tour of East Africa.

Mombasa seemed to be a very cosmopolitan town, with people from all nations, living and working there. The town itself had been gaily decorated for the visit, including an archway of elephant tusks. Something that would not be allowed today. The yacht was guarded by Askaris in khaki uniforms with red fez's, who addressed us in the unfamiliar term of 'Bwana'. H.R.H. arrived on the 22nd September, and we set sail the following day for Port Lois Mauritius, a voyage only broken by a 'ban yan' taken on some coral islands around the Seychelles. Our arrival at Mauritius was great and our subsequent exploration of the island revealed that it was a place of great history and very, very beautiful with its mountains and wonderful beaches. Then there was the Woodbine Race Track. Reputed to be the oldest horse race track known.

Our next port of call was to be Zanzibar but during the time at sea while getting there, it was organised to treat H.R.H. to one of our famous 'Sods Operas'. As far as I can remember this show was 'Cinders at Sea!'. As usual we were taking part with our skiffle group, billed as The Red Sextet, fresh from their Caribbean tour, referring of course to H.R.H. Princess Margaret's trip of solace to the West Indies. There was a departure from the usual cast in the form of a comedy act by a truly crazy character Yeoman Dicky Dilenty who was to appear as an escapologist. During the first half of the show he was seen to be bound in chains and covered with a sack. The audience was expecting him to escape quickly, but not so, after a few minutes the curtain came down with him still struggling. Of course it was all part of the act, and prior to the introduction of each consequent act Dicky was shown still to be struggling on stage when the curtain went up, only to be dragged off each time.

During the evening as I was coming out of the laundry, waiting my turn to go on, Dicky came stumbling down the ladder still bound in his chains. There was not much time between acts to get in and out of them each time. He said 'Charlie just the man I wanted to see, as I desperately want to have a pee!' 'Well I'm not getting your willy out for you I said!' 'No, no just undo the chains you idiot!'

One of the jobs that Dicky liked to do was to keep the signal flags in good repair. And he would work away on his sewing machine with great skill, tucked away in his little workshop below deck. I found out why he was so keen, for it was situated alongside the lower end of the 'Dumb Waiter' that brought the meals from the royal galley to the waiters who served the Royal household staff in their dining room. Dicky would occasionally purloin a main meal, known as 'No 1', and when the waiter asked; 'Where is my No 1?' The chef would call down and say; you have had your No 1 and so the verbal would continue, and our Dicky would be stuffing himself with excellent grub in his little room, all the time laughing at the chef's rising anger.

We arrived at Zanzibar early in the morning, and after anchoring were completely surrounded by an immense shoal of Portuguese jelly fish who managed to kick up quite a stink. Shore leave was given, and the town resembled Tangier with its bazaars. I think the only thing I bought there was a small ivory elephants head that consequently turned out to be not ivory but a piece of bone! I nevertheless kept it for a good many years hanging on the wall at home, until the large ears fell off, whereas it was consigned to a dark and lonely place.

After Zanzibar, we pushed on to Dar-es-Salaam, the last port of call for us, and where H.R.H. left the yacht to continue the East African tour inland. After that it was a return journey to Mombasa. H.R.H. Prince Philip was not due to arrive for a week so it was decided to give each half of the yacht's crew three days leave. There were two options for the leave. One was a stay at the 'Toc-H' club at Silversands, which was an Army rest centre. The Army being very much in evidence, for the terrible 'Mau-Mau' was still a big threat in Kenya. 'Mau-Mau' is often forgotten about these days but was a bad business. In their desire to get independence, the natives sworn to allegiance usually by threats, would go around the countryside killing European farmers etc, men, women and children and horribly mutilating them with their long knives on the orders of a ghastly character by the name of Jomo Kenyatta. There again nothing in Africa changes as far as that is concerned. Even now their independence doesn't seemed to have lifted them to the dizzy height's they were expecting.

The second option for the three day leave was to go on Safari. You don't need a crystal ball to know what idiot volunteered for that one? In actual fact it turned out a fantastic adventure. Our group was to travel in a single decker bus, three hundred miles inland to the Ol Tukai Lodge in the Amboseli National Reserve. This was on the Kenya Tanzania border, in the shadow of Mount Kilimanjaro. Having no knowledge of travelling in Africa, we dressed ourselves in smart uniform, white shorts and tops. No one told us that there were big gaps in the floorboards of the bus, as a result it wasn't very long

Safari transport and living accommodation

before we were all covered in the red dust that came up through the boards. It was very exciting to see all the wild animals on the journey, the only disappointment was that the Amboseli lakes we expected to see were as dry as a bone. In fact the bus drove across them! Even more disappointing to one of our group who had actually brought a fishing rod! After a long, dry, hot and dusty drive, we finally arrived at Ol Tukai Lodge in the early evening, and were very surprised to find that the staff had been busy for quite some time boiling up water for us to have a bath. There was a bathhouse with a number of baths, the water was heated by fires underneath forty gallon oil drums, the heated water would rise through pipes, into a large tank on the roof of the bathhouse. The baths were a godsend, the only trouble was that the insects seemed to like having their bath in the tank on the roof, so when you turned on the taps to fill your bath a generous quota of horrible things felt like joining you for a wash! This had to be overcome by scooping them off the top of the water before getting in. I can tell you that for us sailors who had been a bit pampered, it was a bit of a culture shock.

I will now try to familiarise you with the layout of the Lodge that was to be our home for the next three days. The centre was a large thatched building that was the dining room, kitchens and general get together in the evening sort of thing. There was only half a wall surrounding it, for coolness. Gathered around this building were about a dozen or more small mud walled thatched huts, that accommodated two people in each with nice comfortable beds, complete with mosquito nets and hand basins. The only drawback came in the form of bats living in the thatched roofs and their droppings would fall on your net and roll down onto the floor.

One had to inspect the bed, by pulling back the bedclothes, for it seems that horrible crawly things like the comfort of a nice soft bed as much as we do. On one occasion a poisonous looking, large spider was found curled up, looking ready to defend his chosen place. In addition to these huts was the bathhouse and the water tower that proved to be a magnet to elephants. They could smell the water but could not reach, they had managed in the past to push the water tower over. Finally there was the food store. A strongly built hut, with wire mesh covering the windows, to let an airflow around the food stores that we had brought with us. We had to cook our own food on the wood-burning stoves in the main dining hut previously mentioned. This store hut was also a great attraction to the wild animals, especially monkeys. During the evenings there would be large bonfires lit at each end of the camp to ward off any curious animals. Even so, while on our short journeys between the different huts I began to worry, for there was nothing to stop a brave lion nipping in and carrying you off! 'Anyone seen Charlie Saxby this morning?' Our first night sleeping in the huts was quite traumatic, as during the night laughing hyenas were snuffling around outside making a lot of noise. But the heat of the situation was removed when one of our party a couple of huts away bellowed 'Piss off you black muzzled b******s' Everyone collapsed into laughter, I suppose you could get used to that environment. When we awoke in the morning, to our surprise, there were mounds of elephant dung amongst the huts. We were told that they did roam around because of the water. What if they collide with the huts that we were sleeping in we asked. 'Oh! they sometimes knock them over' was the reply. Say no more.

The following days were taken up in trips on our bus into the surrounding savannah to view the animals. It was just amazing, and on one occasion, a rhino, having had its escape route cut off by the bus, decided to charge and hit the bus with an almighty whack. Some of the lads on that side were shouting 'Torpedo on the port side.' and pretending to climb up on to the luggage rack. On another occasion we saw hundreds of baboons that looked like a huge pack of dogs racing across the open plain. Fortunately they were going away from us.

One of the highlights was meeting a group of Masai warriors guarding their precious cattle. Dressed in their bright red robes and armed with spears and long knives, they looked quite ferocious. One of the younger ones recently had undergone his initiation; part of which was his circumcision, which was attracting quite a lot of flies in that area of his body. Not a pretty sight. All in all it was a great adventure for us, the only thing that marred the whole event was that although we had been warned not to leave the door of the store room open some idiot did. The result was that the monkeys wrecked the place leaving us with next to nothing in the way of food and this was the day before we returned to the yacht. The return journey was to be a hungry one for everybody. We did stop in a village, and the guys bought some packets of biscuits but on opening them saw they were full of weevils.

We finally arrived back at the jetty in Mombasa and staggered out hungry, dirty and shattered but feeling great at what we had experienced. There was another surprise that greeted us. Berthed right behind the yacht was a Castle Line ship carrying hundreds of emigrants from England on a ten pound assisted passage to Australia. Apparently it had arrived the day after we left. The lads had been having a high old time going to parties thrown on the liner. When I went into the laundry to show my face, I found it was full of women working in the laundry, slaving away like hell just for the fun of it while our crew was sitting back drinking beer!

The liner had a large laundry, I suppose the ladies from there wanted to boast at some time or other that they had been in the Royal laundry, and the free beer of course. Even though we had missed the camaraderie and the high jinks while away on the safari, I know which I preferred. Nothing could beat coming out of those huts in the morning and viewing those somewhat dry, but splendid plains. And nothing could match the breathtaking sight of the snowcapped Kilimanjaro in the distance. That now was behind us, and we were back in business as H.R.H. Prince Philip had arrived ready to start his World Tour! We left Mombasa on the 16th October 1956 bound for the Seychelles which was to be the first stop in our voyage. We were consequently to visit Colombo, Trincomalee, Langkawi, Penang, Port Swettenham, Port Moresby, Brisbane, Sydney, Melbourne, Port Lyttleton, Waitangi, Chatham Islands, Antarctica, South Georgia, Falklands.

We arrived at Mahe, Seychelles, this being the largest of the islands of which there are quite a few. Mahe has been known as the original Garden of Eden, with the wonderful thick vegetation that grows on the islands. Helped along by the forbidden fruit Coco der Mer which is a double coconut that looks like ones rear end! In those far off days Seychelles was a tourist location waiting to happen. At that time there was no airfield and a ship would call with supplies once every three months. Another strange statistic was that women outnumbered the men by seven to one! Not bad for the men, not so good for the women.

This all changed when the Royal Air Force was allowed to build an operational airfield there. After that the Garden of Eden was no more. Tourists were arriving and inhabitants were leaving for the big wide world! A big attraction was that in the centre of the town, there was an enclosure containing a number of the largest tortoise I have ever seen. They must have been nearly a metre high, and reputed to be hundreds of years old. I often wonder if they are still there. But then the tortoise were not the only things to be captive at that particular time.

Also interned on the island was Archbishop Makarios, the instigator of all the violence that was taking place in Cyprus. All that was done once again in the name of independence. I am sure in this day and age constant talk would have been just as effective but they wanted it the hard way. They won in the end, only to be invaded by the Turks some years later; back to square one. The British Government had sent Makarios to Seychelles in the hope of quietening things down in Cyprus but unfortunately that didn't work. I only wish that someone would intern me on the island, who would want to come back? But of course that's not quite true, for I was recently married, and had applied for naval married quarters on our return from this voyage.

Unfortunately our stay was very short, and we were soon on our way to the next port of call; Ceylon, or Sri Lanka as it is now known. Another lost colony that has been in terrible trouble ever since. It was the first time that I had been to Sri Lanka and I must say the only thing that impressed me was the gold encrusted temples. Apart from that it was a place that people seemed happy to live in the same old way they had done for centuries and all the streets seemed to be covered in the red dye from the beetle nut they constantly chew and spit the juice everywhere!

We went on to visit Penang, and Port Swettenham in Malaya. As these were only short visits nothing untoward happened to me that was of great interest, except that the more tropical it got, the more arduous it became in the laundry. Sometimes reaching 120 degrees! We had to drink a lot of beer to combat the perspiration! The routine was to work like mad on your twelve hour shift, and then relax on your day off by sunbathing using the temporary swimming pool etc, but nothing too strenuous.

The next port of call was to be Port Moresby in Papua, New Guinea. I didn't know it at the time but apparently Prince Philip was in charge of bringing the yacht in to the berth, through the dangerous channels that were there. We were working away in the bowels of the yacht and knew nothing of this, if we had, I am sure we would have been a bit nervous. But there, he was a good captain in his day.

I remembered that years before when I was serving on H.M.S. Armada in the Mediterranean Fleet we had to carry out an exercise of transferring oil fuel with H.M.S. Magpie, this being Prince Philip's command. On the completion of the exercise the oil pipe was disconnected from their end and a good deal of oil was spilled all down his ship's side. I can remember even now Philip standing up high on the bridge of his ship, and using a megaphone, telling our Captain that he had better send some ratings over at the first possible opportunity to clean up this filthy f****** mess. I think all of us were a bit shocked at hearing that.

Port Moresby. Three day 'Sing sing'

Port Moresby

Now Port Moresby was a different kettle of fish from everywhere we had visited before. It was a savage country. The native population looked, and were savage. When we arrived, they had just started their 'Sing-sing', this was a celebration dance that was to last three days and nights. All the tribes in Papua had sent people to perform in it. They would continue to dance in all their finery until they dropped in exhaustion, whereby they would be replaced, and so on for three days. The rhythm provided by drums and different sized bamboo, which when banged on the ground end-on gave different deep booming sounds.

All this was in honour of H.R.H.'s visit. The natives had bones through their noses, and magnificent head dresses made from Bird of Paradise feathers. New Guinea being the place where the birds are found.

The day after our arrival, we were invited to observe the 'Sing-sing' that was taking place in a large clearing in the surrounding jungle on the edge of town. I suppose that there were about fifty of us. We had to sit on the ground and watch. At one point however, due to the procedure of the ceremony it was part of the dance for them to rush across the field towards us, waving their spears and yelling, stopping short, then throwing their spears into the ground just in front of us. I can tell you that there were a few of us on our feet ready to skedaddle!

I must quote an observation that one of our officers made on that occasion. He said 'Standing close to the largest circle of dancers. One wondered what was going on behind those curiously painted faces. Were they still hankering after the days, only two generations ago, when the best place for a white man was simmering gently in a pot with his head being reduced to the size of a biggish orange in a hut nearby?' That remark hit the spot.

The Australian authorities would not allow alcohol to be sold to any of the native population. Lemonade yes, alcohol no. So you see, they were a bit suspicious of their manner. After our dance fright we went on to the sports club to regain our composure, and grease our gills. I must say that the Aussies were very generous with their hospitality. And it wasn't long before we were a little bit too greased. After a lot of sing songs, and a refusal to let one person fly us up country the next day to see some plantation or other - I mean it was 'only a journey of four or five hundred miles cobber'.

I suppose it must have been the heat, but I was really smashed. An offer was accepted to go back to someone's place for a steak supper. My 'oppos' bunged me in the back of this small van for the journey, not a good idea to make me feel better. The only trouble was, that the other occupant was a bulldog, who insisted on trying to revive me by constantly licking my face. And in consequence made me feel a lot worse, and left my once clean white uniform covered in paw marks.

The cooking facility at the house was a wood burning stove and when the steaks went on, ugh! that really rolled me over. My 'oppos' laid me out on the grass in the garden that was surrounded by jungle. I can still hear those strange animal noises coming out of the jungle. Maybe they put the dog out there to guard me. I am sure he was only interested in the steaks the same as the other greedy lot!

Our last day at Port Moresby was spent on a visit to the allied forces war cemetery. I wasn't prepared for the depressing sight of so many white crosses. And our hearts went out at the thought of the amount of suffering those boys had to go through, at the hands of the Japanese. The ground around the gravestones was covered not in grass, but a kind of moss. When you stepped onto it; clouds of mosquitoes rose up out of it. Thank goodness we were all made aware of the dangers beforehand, and regularly took our salt and anti-malarial pills every morning.

We left New Guinea very much wiser as to the ways of life in an environment that had been a mystery to quite a few of us before. H.R.H. left the yacht before we sailed, to continue his tour of New Guinea, The next time we were to see him would be in Melbourne, Australia where he was to open the Olympic Games. I had not mentioned it before, but as we were visiting Australia and New Zealand, the navy had drafted a certain number of Aussie and New Zealand officers and ratings onto the yacht as a complimentary gesture to those countries. They had all arrived on board, way back in the previous September, in Portsmouth on a dark and damp day. Hardly an inspiring start to a new adventure. Sailors from all countries are the same, they learn to cope with situations.

There were two ratings designated to our mess deck. One Australian John Young, 'Brigham', one New Zealander Ron Soper. As soon as they were settled in and started to chat, they were asking should they go ashore and view Portsmouth or stay and have supper on board? 'What is for supper?' they asked. Bert Cousins, my 'oppo' replied 'Rabbit Pie'. Of course it wasn't, but the look of horror on their faces was a thing to behold. For they consider rabbits to be vermin. 'Christ!, you don't eat them f****** things do you?' they said. 'That's it, we are definitely going ashore then'.

Bert liked to tease John, and on one occasion while we were all sitting at the table in the mess, Bert kept on looking under the table in John's direction. 'What are you looking for?' asked John. 'I know the marks should be there, on your ankles, but I cannot see them' said Bert, referring to the days when Australia was associated with convicts transported from England. Poor old John used to go potty at his little jokes. But no offence was taken. We still remain friends, and I still write to him in Aussie, and try to keep him up to date. Ron the emu was a very easy guy to get on with.

We were off the next day to Brisbane, via the Cook Straits and the Great Barrier Reef. The Reef is really something and if you stand in the bow of the ship in the dark and look down into the sea it seems to be alive with luminous fish darting out of the way. There was one stop on the way, at Fitzroy

Island. This was to allow crew members a swim in the bay. But there was a rapid change of mind, when the lighthouse keepers came down to warn us that there was a good number of sharks around there! The fishing fleets always went back there to gut and clean their catch. Say no more.

We eventually arrived at the Brisbane River and finally reached our berth at Brisbane proper. Our mail had caught up with us there, so I was due for some happy reading from Pat with all the latest news from home. As the stay was only going to be a short one before we were due to sail for Sydney there was only a limited amount of time for sightseeing. Some of the lads were taken off to visit 'Surfers Paradise', not far from the city. That in itself is strange; for that is where my sister Alice lives now, at a place called Runaway Bay. I am not sure if it is a happy escapist name or a place that was favourite for escaping convicts. Anyway my sister loves it there, and so do the surfers.

Our programme was soon to see us off to sea again bound for Sydney. The reception there was quite loud and enthusiastic even though H.R.H. was not with us as he was still doing his tour of New Guinea. Our berth was to be at a place called Garden Island, Woolamaloo. Admiral Connolly Able Smith brought the yacht in so fast that everyone was convinced that there was going to be an almighty crash but in his usual style, he reversed the engines at a perfect time and brought us into our berth with the greatest of ease. Sir Connolly was a great old chap. I remember some years after he had retired the yacht was berthed in Portsmouth for some essential repairs and he paid a surprise visit. I was quartermaster on the gangway when he drew up at the bottom in his Land Rover with horse box in tow. Before I had a chance to let the officer of the watch know he was on his way onboard, Sir Connolly had run up the gangway, and he called out to me 'Don't worry Saxby I'll introduce myself.' I was amazed, how did he remember my name? It must have been at least two years since he had left the yacht.

Now Sydney was, and is to this present day a fun city, it seemed to stay awake all night. It is also steeped in history. It was amazing to see how many of the houses had wrought iron balconies, being a survivor from Victorian times. All the wrought iron had gone from England long ago when the government removed it all at the beginning of the war to use for armament manufacture.

Sydney was also the Australian naval base, so the ratings we had on board knew all the best places to go and drink They were to set the itinerary that our lads were only too happy to follow. First stop the Rendezvous Cafe for big eats. The Rendezvous was crudely referred to by the Aussies as, and I quote 'the chew and spew'. After having a good feed there, they would move on to Kings Cross, that seemed to have all the best pubs. They did have the same opening hours as in the U.K. but if more drinking was required, all you had to do was to go into a hotel and order a sandwich, and then you could drink all night if you wanted to. Also the cinemas stayed open all night. During the day one could visit the Taronga Park Zoo, which I did. The population was great, mostly very friendly, with a great sense of humour.

On one occasion, I was returning to the yacht after drinking with some of the lads and my route home was by way of the Sydney Harbour Bridge. A taxi drew up alongside me to enquire if I wanted a ride. I said to him 'Sorry mate I have no money left for taxis.' He said 'How much have you got?' 'One and ninepence' I replied. 'Jump in,' he said, 'If I take any more of you Pommies back tonight for that amount, I will go bankrupt, don't they pay you enough in your Navy?' He then drove me all the way back to Woolamaloo, to the accompaniment of verbal fencing between the two of us. So that is the cheapest taxi fare I have ever had.

Soon it was time to leave Sydney and take the long trip down the east coast to Melbourne, where we were due to join up with H.R.H. We had made good use of our time in Sydney to clean and spruce up the yacht for our big entry to Melbourne and the Olympic Games. I was particularly looking forward to our visit, for as mentioned at the beginning of these memoirs, my Dad's brother Arthur emigrated for a new life in Australia all those years ago. Now at long last I was to meet his son; my cousin and his family for the first time. Rex and his wife Nancy, had expanded the Saxby family by three sons and one daughter at the time I met them, Rex was still in the army, a Warrant Officer no less. He had served in Vietnam along with the Americans as a supply officer.

We arrived at Port Melbourne, and made the long journey up the Yarra River to finally berth at the Spencer Street Bridge. The provisions for our stay had been well organised, for they had supplied us with television sets to watch the games. There were plenty of complimentary tickets for anyone who wanted to go and watch the events. I had been granted four days leave to spend with my cousin Rex and his family. We had been in contact by mail for some time before I arrived at Melbourne, and following the instructions given me by letter, I was to catch the train at Flinders St. Station, for East Camberwell, and from there a short walk to their bungalow.

The train journey was an eye opener, for it was quite obvious that the English influence was there for the train stations made you feel you were travelling in Kent. They were so much alike, even to the potted plants on the platforms. There was some differences, in as much as the seats in the train were constructed of wooden slats. The object being to avert the nasty little creepy crawly things you get in semi-tropical climates. The other occupants of the carriage I was in were a 'no hoper tramp' who gave off a delicate aroma, that was strong enough to make you gag. The other was a little old lady, who never removed her lavender scented handkerchief from her nose the whole time the 'no hoper' was in the carriage.

After completing the journey I found the bungalow with Nancy and the children who were of course expecting me. Rex had yet to arrive, so at the appointed time of his arrival I went with the kids to the station to meet him. It was a strange meeting for both of us, a bit tense and reserved, but over the next few days all that disappeared for we all got on famously. The room I had was situated alongside a large tree that was a favourite spot for a kookaburra, who every morning perched itself, and let rip with its call that sounded like a lunatic laughing. At one point, Rex got me up 'very' early to take me on a long drive to see the sun come up over the dam. It was well worth seeing, we also had breakfast at his friends log cabin. Steaming hot coffee, followed by devilled kidneys on fried bread, 'lovely'. I didn't mind him getting me up on occasions such as that.

The other trip he insisted on, was a fishing trip with a friend of his. The day started with the usual break of dawn departure, in Rex's friend's open back truck. I have no idea why I was going, for the only thing I knew about fishing was that you would put something on the hook, throw the hook in the water, and hope that a passing fish would be stupid enough to try and swallow it. The asphalt roads soon disappear along the outer edges of Melbourne, then you are left with hundreds of miles of dirt roads. We seemed to be travelling for ages, and on seeing some kangaroos Rex and his pal said that they must be from the kangaroo farm just down the road. They both convulsed in laughter. An inside Australian joke I supposed.

We arrived at a river that could only be reached by crossing some fenced-in pasture land containing an enormous amount of cattle. They both cheered me up by telling me to keep an eye out for the deadly tiger snakes. So when a flock of small birds jumped up out of the grass being disturbed by our approach, I thought my time had come, and my heart seemed to be in my mouth. The cattle suddenly took an interest in our invasion of their space. Rex said not to worry, as they were only inquisitive creatures, that is until they all broke into a mad stampede to get to us, which forced us to run for our lives to the opposite fences for fear of being trampled.

When we finally reached the river, that originated in the nearby hills, I was obliged to climb up a waterfall, the best place to catch fish apparently. We gradually moved down the river 'fly fishing' My concentration was not so much on catching anything, but more on staying out of the river, and not being dispatched by a tiger snake, when I suddenly realised that I was alone. They had rounded the bend and gone. The other thing they had warned me about was the soft 'quicksand' patches that surrounded the river. Having realised I could no longer tread in their experienced footsteps, I decided that I had done enough fishing, and very carefully retraced my steps, treading on the biggest lumps of grass I could find, and across the field while the cattle seemed not to be looking, and parked myself in the truck, after throwing the fishing rod into the back. I must say that I much preferred watching the sun rise and eating breakfasts in log cabins!

The rest of my stay with my family was spent on sightseeing with them around the town. Also after trips to the local liqueur store to replenish the supply of 'tinnies', the evenings were spent playing board games. The favourite was, 'Monopoly', which although enjoyed, managed to get a bit too competitive. One particular game, Nancy found herself heavily in debt to me, unable to meet her debt, she had to go bankrupt. They all got upset because I would not let her off the hook! Many years later: Alan, who was the eldest of the boys, having succeeded in forming a strawberry exporting business, was in England for meetings and paid a visit to us in Gawber St. He surprised me by giving me the exact amount in 'Monopoly money' that she owed me on that night back in East Camberwell! Great sense of humour. Nancy had also given him a coat hanger to pass on to me that I had inadvertently left there on my visit. It was a rather posh coat hanger, and she had no idea it was one that I had purloined from the Queen's apartments on the yacht! I think she would have kept it had she known. Anyway it was returned to me and I still have it now.

Now the Olympic Games was at an end, so to was our time at Melbourne. Although the farewell to Rex and his family was sad, it was not the last time I was to see them, for Alan brought them over to England for a visit to the old country.

I feel that I must digress a little bit from the main theme of the story, by relating an account of what happened on one occasion when Alan was in England on business. It had been arranged that he would stay with us at Gawber St. It was also arranged that he was to go to Portsmouth, with Pat and I along with daughter Diane for the weekend, to attend my reunion dinner for the Royal Yacht.

We stayed at our usual place the Sailors Home Club. This was an establishment with very humble beginnings as a short stay, doss down place for naval personnel when ashore. But now had become a very nice hotel, once again for naval families. When we were gathered in the bar that evening prior to me going to the dinner, we were joined by many former ex-yachtsmen, one of whom gave his ticket to Alan to enable him to attend the dinner with me. Totally illegal, but there you are. We had the meal, during which we listened to the speech by Prince Edward, who was the Royal guest of honour for that evening.

After the dinner, we all retired to the bar for some noisy talk on past memories and catching up on each other's lives after the yacht. I was surprised when I heard Alan calling me over to have a chat with Prince Edward, who he had managed to corner in conversation in God knows what subject, probably strawberries. The cheek of it all. Alan had quite a few attributes, one of them was keeping his ear to the ground so during the evening he had heard that Keith Humphries, ex-yachtie, and now the manager of the Victory Shop situated in the dockyard, was organising a party on board the H.M.S. Victory no less. So on Saturday morning we popped down to see him, and managed to fiddle ourselves onto the guest list.

We had a great time that evening, but it was very strange to be on Nelson's flagship, drinking and making merry, knowing that all those years ago, hundreds of men had fought and died in the very same place. But Alan disgraced himself that night by drawing a bubble on the glass front of Lord Nelson's picture with the words 'you must be joking'. A truly cardinal sin, that was to be my undoing. After the weekend, I returned to work at the London Rubber Company. Having parked my car, I turned to walk away when there was such a pain in my left leg that I thought I had been shot. It turned out that I had snapped some muscles, and spent the next three weeks in hospital. During which time I was taken to an auditorium, where the doctor in charge of my case explained to the gathering of doctors the details of my troublesome leg.

When he finished his explanation he said 'That's my theory now Mr Saxby will tell you his.' So I told them about Alan's drawing on Nelson's picture, and in retaliation Nelson's spirit had kicked me in the leg for letting it happen, and the doctors let out a roar of laughter.

So having sampled the delights of Australia we left Melbourne en route for Port Lyttleton, New Zealand. We arrived there on a very windy day, and in the process of securing alongside the oiling jetty, were blown heavily onto the said jetty causing damage to the yacht's side. Port Lyttleton was the port for Christchurch. To reach it took a journey on a train under a mountain range via a tunnel. The train was just like those you see in the cowboy films, with little open areas on the end of the carriages. When going through the tunnel the smoke from the engine would blow right through the carriages.

We were only to stay at New Zealand for two days, but in that time it was possible to test out the beer in their pubs that were so much like ours in England. Unlike the ones in Aussie that had no seats and walls and floors were tiled and sawdusted. The beer there would be delivered to your glass via a hose and gun attachment, the spillage was intense. Not only that but the bars opened at five o'clock, and closed at six! That was to make sure the guys didn't spend all their money and time there before they arrived home! Needless to say, they got as much beer down themselves as they could in that one hour. New Zealand's pubs although being comfortable also had funny opening times. Also three sizes of glasses for the amount of beer you required. The best treat of all was the steak restaurants, where you would get a huge steak for the minimal amount of money, lovely.

As I said, the stay was not long, and we were soon off on to our next stop Chatham Islands a New Zealand dependency. Another short stay that included a whacky horse race, and a huge barbecue of lamb being spitted and served at the end of the race, along with good beer. Our departure from the islands was to herald our next great adventure, the Antarctic.

Our voyage was to take us south across the South Pacific, around Cape Horn, Argentina, onto Graham Land, and the South Shetland Admiralty Bay, to visit the British Antarctic expeditionary bases. At this point I would like to quote an official report given after the events:

"We were well and truly into the Roaring Forties and all prepared for south west gales, mountainous seas and driving rain. We looked out our oilskins and sea boots, lashed the suitcases on top of the lockers and waited with a towel handy to go around the neck. We waited for the call to secure a piece of equipment which had broken loose, to secure it in driving greenwater and on a wildly heaving deck. We waited with some apprehension to oil at sea in conditions where the hose lashes like a wild thing, where ropes are wet and raw to the hands and the spray falls with monotonous regularity on a streaming and slippery deck. We waited but to everyone's relief in vain."

The reason could only be put down to the fact that the Admiral had been given a special green stone by the lady Maori Mayoress on Chatham Islands. This special stone was purported to bring good luck to a voyage. It certainly seemed to have worked for us, as we had a wonderful journey southwards. The sea was calm and the weather bright, you would have thought we were in the Mediterranean.

As we had left the Chatham Islands on the 19th December we were destined to reach a halfway point between the Islands and Cape Horn on Christmas Day, so there was plenty of time to decorate the messes, and arrange the festive dinner. It. seems strange now that we could be doing all those things in the relative comfort of our surroundings, at least twelve hundred miles from the nearest land. H.R.H. was going to give a Christmas speech from the yacht to the U.K. through various means all worked out a long time previously. This took place at 6.55am our time but afternoon U.K. time. I remember waking up and listening to it from the comfort of my hammock, and feeling very impressed by the fact that it was leaving the yacht, going all the way home and coming back to us so that the words were slightly echoed.

All in all it was a good Christmas, plenty to eat and drink, the drink consumed during the lunch took effect during the afternoon. Someone instigated a conga line, that grew with great rapidity that it was joined by officers and men alike. It weaved its way down to the Royal Apartments looking for H.R.H. the Duke of Edinburgh to join in the fun. We looked but could not find him, until someone spotted him on the end of the line. It seemed that all protocol had been thrown aside.

Other events were a party given in the stewards mess, and singalongs. There is no doubt that it was the most collective and enjoyable Christmas I have had. The Duke had given it a personal touch by visiting the messes and awarding a prize for the best decorated. He was also given a Christmas present by one of the messes in the form of a well wrapped parcel, that when he finally managed to get through the many layers of paper, found it to be a brand new razor! This was an inside joke, for he wanted to grow a beard to look the part for the Antarctic so he had called for a beard growing contest, that would mean everyone would for a time look scruffy.

Boxing Day was a bit hazy, but nonetheless efficient. We saw our first iceberg during the forenoon, and were informed that it was three miles long and one hundred and fifty feet high, some iceberg. This was followed by a snowstorm, a sure sign that we were approaching the serious stuff. Later on during the day, we met up with the 'Southern Harvester' the factory whaling ship.

H.R.H. was transferred onto a whale catcher that used one of the whales it had caught as a fender in between their ship and ours. He then went onto visit the factory ship. The smell coming from it was very strong, so that even at that distance we could whiff it. History was being made at this time, for we had now crossed the Antarctic Circle, and in doing so, the two lady secretaries, Miss Stevenson and Miss Eadie who had been with us from the beginning, (Sorry not to have mentioned them before) were the first British ladies ever to cross the Antarctic Circle.

On one occasion when Miss Eadie was climbing through a small hatchway to reach the upper deck, she hesitated halfway through to get her bearings. The result was for the air updraught to lift her

The beaches of Antarctica

beautiful red dress and flatten it against the underside of the hatch, revealing all to the sailors who were waiting below to use the same hatchway! There was a lot of looking going on for the period that she was standing in that position!

There were even more surprises when we finally reached the British expedition base at Admiralty Bay, for unknown to the guys manning the base, who had been there for two years, the visiting party of H.R.H. included two ladies. These men had not seen any females for all that time, and they were falling over themselves in their attempts to be the perfect hosts. I and others also visited, but did not get the same attention, ha, ha.

New Year's Day, we met up with the 'John Biscoe', this was the Falkland Islands Dependency Survey vessel, She was built for ice conditions, and would be our scout ship, leading the way to make sure we did not hit any 'bergie bits', and also to take H.R.H. into the various British and foreign bases which were inaccessible to us.

Seeing the ice for the first time is a most remarkable sight. One would imagine just pure white,

Admiralty Bay. I could not resist posing for these shots

but if you are lucky enough to have the sun shining as we did, you would see a myriad of reflected colours of the rainbow, 'chromatic apparition' when the sun shone through the ice and into the cave like hollows. Now you must remember that all this time I had been employed in my job in the laundry, well protected from the cold and inclement weather that the other lads had to suffer.

Now we were really into the Antarctic I decided to go up top and have a good look around. I donned my duffel coat, plus the other cold weather gear and stepped onto the deck. I was not prepared for the low air pressure and was a bit concerned when I thought my ears were going to pop out. But it didn't take long to acclimatise. Shortly afterwards I was lucky enough to go ashore and visit the British base, along with my 'oppos' Bert Cousins and Darby Allen. We were given tea and cakes in the cosy wooden base huts and afterwards messed about waist deep in snow, watching the masses of penguins. The teams of Husky dogs caught our attention but were put off stroking them when we were advised not to if we wanted to keep all our fingers.

There were other opportunities to go ashore at places of great interest such as the King Penguin breeding colony and the elephant seals. Elephant seals are of immense size, probably weighing a ton or more. We were advised not to stand in front of them as they had a nasty habit of flicking their tails right over their head and squashing you in the process. Definitely a defence move! The King Penguins defence was to spit a foul smelling liquid at you if you felt the need to chase and pick one up! The thing that shocked me while visiting these areas was the amount of whale bones that littered the shoreline, they were everywhere, giant jaw bones, vertebrae, just about every part of the body. We were to be even more shocked later on for we had to accompany a whale catcher stalking a whale and killing it with the harpoon. This was done with the Duke aboard the catcher observing the procedure. But for now our tour of the Antarctic shelf was done, and our next port of call was Port Stanley, Falkland Islands.

Our arrival at Port Stanley was greeted with the usual enthusiasm we had grown to expect. Falklands was a very bland sort of place, no trees only flat land covered with a mossy grass and peaty soil. Wonderful for the large sheep flocks and plentiful hares that abounded there. What was interesting was the fact that the S.S. Great Britain was berthed there and was being used as a coal storage hulk for the population of Port Stanley. She was Britain's first all iron ship that had ended up here and was now no more than a hulk. The good news though, is that many years later, it was brought back to England on a giant raft was fully restored to its former glory, and is now on display at Bristol, Hooray!

H.R.H. visiting the Shackleton memorial in South Georgia

     The entertainment they had arranged for us was varied, it included a horse race that was like the one in Chatham Islands. The only difference was, that the norm was to tank up the riders with a good deal of drink, to see who managed to remain on their mount at the end of the course! There was an old time dance. Also the dubious opportunities of joining hare shooting parties. I don't think it would be necessary to tell you who was well up for that, as he is quite well known for his liking of blood sports.

Whaling Base South Georgia; they dispose of a whale this size in twenty minutes

The Falklands was clear of snow this time of year, as it was a lot nearer Cape Horn, Argentina. That was not the case of our next destination, South Georgia.

For a run down on Georgia it is a completely uninviting, desperate place, that has no inhabitants, except for the two whaling stations. It is covered in ice and snow most of the time. There is some history, the great explorer Shackleton's Memorial is there. He performed a most amazing feat. After his ship foundered in the ice at the beginning of an exploration he managed to get his crew to Elephant Island, where he left them while he himself set out on an almost impossible sea trip to Georgia. He made a landfall, but on the wrong side of the island. After climbing the mountain range, he and his companions slid down a glacier for two thousand feet to the whaling station. They organised a rescue ship, and went back to Elephant Island to get the rest of his crew. Of course the other bit of history is that Georgia is the place that the Falkland War began, after the Argentinians, on the pretence of demolishing the whaling station there landed troops and invaded the Falkland Isles.

The only activities that happened there as far as we were concerned, was the playing of a football match, and when we went ashore, en masse, to watch the processing of the ninety ton whale that H.R.H. had been involved with while on the whale catcher previously. It was cut up into smaller pieces in a remarkable forty minutes, and processed into the boiling pots. I must point out that the whole place stank horribly, and I wasn't able to get the smell out of my nose for quite some time afterwards.

The icebergs around the island were numerous, and at one point thirty-six were counted in one particular sighting operation. In fact, on our way to Georgia one was estimated as being five miles long and one mile wide. They don't do things by half out there.

On the 12th of January we left Georgia having completed our Antarctic journey over great distances since leaving the Chatham Islands. All of it had taken just eighteen days. Now for the first time in months 'Britannia' turned her bow in the direction of home. The only other visits would be Gough Island, Tristan-da-Cunha, St. Helena, Ascension Island, Bathurst in Gambia, Gibraltar then finally Lisbon to meet up with H.M. the Queen, for her state visit to Portugal, England's oldest ally. You see we still had a lot to do, but at least we were going in the right direction.

We now had to cross the South Atlantic, and having the reputation that it has, we all hoped that the skipper was still rubbing that green stone as hard as he could. The Maori good luck charm had served us remarkably well so far.

Gough Island turned out to be quite small, the only inhabitants being crew manning the Meteorological Station. It seemed that we had arrived just in time, for one of the lads there had been taken ill. He was brought aboard, and when examined by the two surgeon commanders was found to have acute appendicitis. As I mentioned at the beginning the yacht was equipped with a fully functional operating theatre and he was operated on that night and left with us the next morning.

I had on one occasion to visit the sick bay with a worrying grey, furry tongue. When examined

Whale catcher coming alongside using a whale as fender

by Surgeon Commander Burgess, he said that as I was working below deck for such long periods I was liverish, and that I should drink plenty of 'red goffer' this being made up of lemonade that you purchased at the canteen by the glassful. I was naturally curious, and asked what good that would do? He said 'None at all, but it would change the horrible colour of that tongue', you can't help laughing can you?

The next port of call was, Tristan-da-Cunha. Now this is a really interesting island, rugged mountain terrain overshadowed by an extinct volcano or so everybody thought. It is occupied by a few hundred people who are completely self reliant with plenty of sheep, cattle and agriculture but very strange people indeed. All descendants of shipwrecked sailors, and a controlled inbreeding of third cousins. Being isolated as they were, their old fashioned customs, and homespun clothes, were a very unusual sight. It was a shame that our stay could not have been longer, but the anchorage was a bit iffy, and could not be trusted if the weather turned sour. Some years later the volcano did erupt, and all the islanders had to be rescued. After a few years of living in England they were all returned back to their island home.

About this time, we had our judgement of who had grown the best beard. There was a lot of dressing up to bring as much humour into it as possible. Needless to say it wasn't me who won, but I did not do too badly. There were some of the lads that grew so much, they resembled gorillas, but one lad received the booby prize, he grew just one hair but quite long. Also at this time we received our Antarctic Red Nose Certificates. These certificates were the brainchild of the Duke who had designed and made them himself, no doubt with able assistance. They were made with a system called lino-cuts specifically to commemorate our journey across Antarctica.

It seems now that we were using the islands like railway stations. But that was not the case, for we were paying our respects at each place. The next stop was to be St. Helena but during the night we had an emergency call from the S.S. Mabel Ryan, who had a sick man on board, so we diverted and met the ship and took the man aboard. On examination he was found to have, you've guessed it, acute appendicitis, he was operated on successfully. Well 'Britannia' was meant to be a hospital ship if called for.

Finally we arrived at Jamestown, St. Helena, what a wonderful place this is, full of intrigue and history. Its beginnings are associated with pirates, lost seamen, and above all this is where Napoleon Bonaparte was exiled after his escape from Elba. Also the place where he eventually died. Napoleon had a house called Longwood on the highest point above the town, which was reached on foot by a near vertical stone stairway comprising of 699 steps! The young lads for a few coins would slide all the way down for your amusement, and of course to show off. The house is still there on the top of the hill and also 'Bonies' grave, but he is not in it. The French, removed him years ago and reburied him in Paris, but Longwood is a very popular tourists attraction nowadays.

H.R.H. Prince Philip cutting the original lino-cut that produced the certificates

It's strange how St. Helena was to affect part of my life in later years for one of my 'oppos' 'Buster' Brown met and married a nurse who came from St. Helena. After he had served his time in the navy they both returned to St. Helena to settle down. I heard that he was doing very well and was a pillar of the society. Then when Philip, my son died, the Bishop that was performing the burial ceremony also came from St. Helena and knew 'Buster' quite well, he also remembered our visit to the island, all those years ago.

But once again it was to be a short stopover, and we were soon on our way. After a three day voyage we made a brief stop at Ascension Islands more to take on water than anything else to see us through on our long leg, across the South Atlantic to Africa and our long planned visit to Bathurst in Gambia. This was to be the last stop of Philip's world tour, before we moved over to Gibraltar to preen ourselves, and make sure the yacht looked her best, for H.M. the Queen's official tour of Portugal.

The trip from Ascension Islands to Gambia took four days, and across the Equator for the fourth time since the beginning of the tour. This meant that we had left the snow and icebergs far behind and were now back into all white tropical uniforms. Of course this put the laundry on double work load. The temperature climbed again into the 120 degrees mark. We would start work in the morning in crisp white trousers and tee shirt, but in a very short time would be clammy and wet. But as I have mentioned before, I enjoyed the work a great deal and also had a great sense of achievement. It was officially documented at the end of the cruise that we had dhobied over 30 tons of laundry of all types, Wow!

We entered the River Gambia, and moved up to Sankwia, and dropped anchor. The reason for the visit was for H.R.H. to attend a meeting of chiefs there. We, the crew were allowed ashore to see a display of native dancing, and some dancing camels, one of which fell over during its excited performance, much to the amusement of us ignorant matelots. There was another time filler while H.R.H. completed his duties and that was the offer of taking part in a crocodile hunt. Of course like the idiot I am, I put my name down right away thinking it would be a highly organised occasion.

What it actually turned out to be was that the two jollyboats, with an officer in charge, along with the volunteers, going off in different directions, to find their own mangrove tributary to explore and look for the odd crocodile to shoot! There was no expert to accompany us, as they were all busy looking after H.R.H. We entered our chosen tributary, and was immediately shocked to find a giant eleven foot monster of a crocodile poised on a sandy bank four feet above the level of our boat! Hold on, this isn't how we had planned it. We all stood there mesmerised until it slid down the bank and into the water with the quickness of a snake. At which point, the rating, me with the 303 rifle, fired into the water after it. Totally useless of course but at least some reaction. After that we slowly continued down the narrowing tributary and were taken by surprise at the number of 'crocs' rushing down the tunnels in the undergrowth to reach the water on hearing our approach. The surrounding trees were full of little red monkeys scampering about. One of the lads suggested that we shoot a few of them to use as bait for the 'crocs'! It turned out no one was willing to do the dirty deed, so that idea was abandoned. We continued on down our ever narrowing tributary, with some of the lads leaning over the side to see if they could catch sight of any lurking 'crocs'. This is a thought that fills me with horror now for having seen on film the way that 'crocs' leap out of the water to catch their prey, I am sure that we were lucky for our inexperienced crocodile trip not to end in disaster. Nonetheless, our progress was brought to a halt when the creek terminated in a very large sandbank that was obviously the place where a large number of 'crocs' basked and did whatever crocodiles do in their spare time. There was not one to be seen. The young Lieutenant who was in charge of the jollyboat concluded that if they were not on the sandbank, then they must be swimming around underneath us. We all looked at one another in hushed silence, it did not need any words to convey what we were feeling. We turned the boat around to retrace our way back! So ended our hunt, I am glad that we did not kill anything, not even each other in our clumsy attempts at being the big bwana.

Looking back now, with a great deal of nostalgia it's strange to see how many things have changed for the wild Gambia that we were introduced to then is now a sought after tourist place, somewhere to take the children on holiday. The world is shrinking.

Before we left Gambia for Gibraltar the government there organised for each member of the ship's company to receive a copy of the chief's meeting with H.R.H. This was in an addressed envelope, that was stamped and franked by the floating Post Office, that plied up and down the River Gambia. Quite an unique memento that I still have today.

So ended our mammoth cruise with the Duke. On to Gibraltar for a big clean and paint up for H.M. the Queen's visit to Portugal. We stayed a total of nine days at Gibraltar, doing all the things that were needed to eradicate the ravages of our epic journey. At the same time enjoying the welcome break. H.R.H. remained with us all this time, the intention being that he arrived with us to join H.M. the Queen at Lisbon.

When things were totted up, besides the laundry doing 30 tons of washing, we found out that we had steamed 39,550 nautical miles, visited 38 ports and 21 different countries! We were all very satisfied.

Our journey from Gibraltar to Setubal, Portugal was a very hairy one indeed, for the weather had turned foul, and we were sailing into a force eight gale. Just the thing to take the shine off our efforts to make the yacht pristine. H.M. the Queen joined the yacht next day at Setubal for a happy reunion with the Duke, after a separation of several months. We then proceeded up river to Lisbon, where H.M. the Queen and H.R.H. were taken ashore in a massive Royal Barge, manned by forty oarsmen, who all rowed in a quick succession of three strokes separated by a short pause, it was a very commanding sight indeed. Apparently there were six thousand troops massed in the square for her to inspect. But I am sure she did not inspect them all! That evening after the banquet H.M. the Queen had attended as guests of Portugal we were treated to the most magnificent firework display I have ever seen. After this the Royals left the yacht to return to England by means that were all pre-arranged. We on the other hand left the next day, and after after a two day sail reached Portsmouth on Sunday, to find five hundred of our families awaiting our arrival at our berth at South Railway Jetty. Pat was there along with her cousin Margaret. They had both travelled down from London for the big occasion, and a very welcome sight indeed. Our circumnavigation of the globe was now over, until next time that is.

Introduction to Domestic Life

After our return we received two weeks leave staggered between the ship's company. Also Pat and I had good news that we were now entitled to a maisonette at the naval estate being built at Rowner, Gosport, on the opposite side of Portsmouth harbour. We were to go and inspect No. 33 Shackleton Rd. Quite odd when you take into account what I previously wrote about Shackleton's Memorial in South Georgia.

Our inspection of the maisonette turned out to be quite exciting. We packed a lunch with a flask of coffee to make a day of it. On our arrival we were surprised to see that the estate was half finished being built across the old navy airfield H.M.S. Sultan. The maisonette turned out to be a cracker, the only drawback was that it was the upstairs one. But then we were young. It was fully furnished, a bit sparse but nonetheless it was to be our first home, and the weekly rent was to be, wait for it, seventeen shillings and sixpence a week, 87.5p in today's money. We sat in the front room looking out of the window at the fields in front of us, it was so quiet and we watched the wild rabbits running about by the hedge, when suddenly there was a low pitched whistle, we looked and searched until completely baffled, and a little anxious about what it could be. We decided to have a cup of coffee and on opening the coffee, the noise stopped. It was only air escaping from the flask. Our mind was made up and we decided to take it after we finished laughing at our consternation.

The decision turned out to be a good one for we were to be surrounded on all sides by members of the yacht's crew, who for the same reasons as ourselves had qualified for naval accommodation. It was to be a great asset, for while we were away on trips the wives always had each other for company, and could watch over each other. Our immediate neighbours were P.O. Steward, John Grace and Joyce, who lived downstairs to us. Darby Allen and Tobi the Scandinavian wife of Darby. She was a brave girl, who moved to England after getting married hardly speaking any English. Next door upstairs to us was a stoker mechanic and his wife. He had a bit of a drinking problem. Nothing new, for I think all stoker mechanics have drinking problems, must be something to do with the hot environment they worked in.

We moved in as soon as we could, and began to adjust to our new lives. The facilities in the flat were all very good and met our every need, but only needed personalising.

The one exception was the gardens, these were shared, one between two flats. Darby and I soon changed the look of the garden. After the builders had finished work for the day, Darby and I would borrow one of their wheelbarrows and pinch lots of grass turfs that were being lifted on the airfield, in the process of building more maisonettes. So in no time at all, we both had a ninety square foot lawn in our own particular garden. We gradually changed our barren rubble strewn gardens into a respectable habitat with flowers etc.

We also had the great pleasure of having our first daughter Lynn at the flat. She was not born there, but at a hospital in the adjacent neighbourhood of Elton. She took us by surprise, when very early in the morning, Pat's water broke, and I had to bundle her into the motorbike sidecar that we had at that time, and very, very carefully drive over bumpy roads to the hospital, about three miles away.

One other thing we had to get used to was the fact, that by living in naval accommodation it was the rule that you went 'R.A.', rationed ashore. This meant that as one no longer had food on board the yacht, they were given an allowance for living at home in the flat. It was just like having a job in 'civvy street', for you would take sandwiches for the day, and have your main meals when you arrived home. We would go home every night, with the exception of when required for duty. This proved a little difficult meal-wise, but then there was always someone that was going ashore, and not requiring their food, problem solved.

All this would take place while we were at our permanent berth at Whale Island, but would be reversed when we went away on Royal duty. The journey from Rowner to Whale Island was quite a long and complex one, involving two bus trips and a ferry trip across the harbour. In view of this, most of us 'R.A.s' purchased some form of transport. No need to guess what I bought, a 250cc B.S.A! This was a small bike that suited the situation, with the one exception, that Pat decided that she would like to learn how to ride it!

Our flat was an ideal place for her to learn for our street was a very quiet backwater, also we had fields to the front and sides. She quickly picked up the rudiments of operating the bike and was soon managing to ride up and down in first gear. But one moment when she became over confident, she lost control of the machine. The bike mounted the kerb, and took off across the field! It was going up and down like mad over the bumpy field, with Pat hanging on, her skirt billowing up in the air, and me running after her, shouting out for her to de-clutch, and to put the brakes on! At last, after some very anxious moments she did do those things, but unfortunately she forgot to put her feet down on the ground. The result was that the bike and Pat toppled over when it came to a standstill. The sad bit was that the exhaust pipe touched her leg, and gave her a nasty burn. If that had not happened, then I think she would have had another go. As it was she was completely put off the idea of riding!

The small bike did not last long before I changed it for a motorbike and sidecar. It was a Triumph Thunderbird and matching sidecar that I nearly wrecked on my first attempt at riding by crashing the sidecar wheel on the kerb. But we were in business, for now we could travel up and down to London without dragging all our belongings onto the train.

There was the time that I took leave of my senses and bought a dog from the then famous Brick Lane pet market. It was supposed to be a spaniel, black and white in colour. But by the time it grew, we realised that it was no more than a mongrel with no more sense than it was born with. It would shed its coat everywhere. On a regular occurrence after I had bathed the little tyke she would find the nearest dirty puddle and roll about in it! The final straw came when Pat came home from shopping to find the fire brigade at our flat rescuing the dog from the window ledge. It was spotted by a passerby, standing on the window ledge all four paws in a straight line trying to keep its balance on the narrow space. How it managed to get out there I really did not know. Fortunately a young lady had taken a shine to the dog, and we quickly offloaded her to a new owner.

So we settled down in our new home, spending time with our neighbours, hosting each other on game nights, playing various board games, and providing refreshments. All in all it was quite pleasant as all the residents were young and healthy, and thinking of extending their families. It still came as a surprise to hear that there were no less than ninety expectant mums in the one main street that ran through the estate! The bus conductors used to call out in fun, when the bus reached Rowner naval estate, 'Rabbit Warren'. Needless to say some were amused, and the more serious were not!

Back to Royal Duty

1958 turned out to be not so exciting as the previous year, but nonetheless a big honour for us all to make H.M. the Queen's visits a great success. The year had started off with a month's work-up period to make sure that everything was in order, plus the new section of the crew that had joined in the change around system to give all in the navy an opportunity to experience Royal Yacht Service 'R.Y.S.'

The work up period was followed with visits by members of the Royal Family to Holland, Ireland, north and south of England. Scotland was by far the most visited for that year. I had been shifted from my job in the laundry after being uprated to Leading Seaman. I was now the Chief Quartermaster. The grand title meant that I was in charge of the staff that manned the gangway and controlled the comings and goings from ship to shore when in harbour. When at sea our job was to man the wheelhouse to steer the ship under the direction of officers on the bridge above the wheelhouse, and to run the daily routine of the ship, again under direction.

There would be three Quartermasters on watch in the wheelhouse at the same time: two to operate the telegraphs that send engine movements to the engine room; one to steer the ship, swopping around at intervals to break the boredom. In front of the steering wheel there were two large brass speaking funnels, to allow the Quartermaster doing the steering to speak to the bridge and repeat the orders given from the bridge.

When we were at sea the people on the bridge would delight in dropping down the funnels every horrible flying insect they found that had landed on the ship for a rest. I can tell you that there were some ghastly looking things such as bats, things with dangerous looking legs and biting things. The bridge staff would drop them down, and then roll about in laughter at the resulting yells and sounds of pandemonium coming up from the wheelhouse! The actual steering of the yacht was slightly boring for there was only a blank bulkhead in front of you. Blank that is with the exception of the 'Gyroscopic Strip' that you steered by, and a very large picture of King George V sailing his yacht 'Britannia'.

You could not see where you were going. I think it was just as well not to see, as the helmsman might decide to steer his own course in a moment of panic. In my stint in the Quartermaster's job, I had a total of two hundred hours on the wheel. In calm weather it was a doddle, with only the minimum of wheel movement, but when it was rough you would have a real battle on your hands, throwing the wheel from one direction to the other to counteract the swing of the ship through the waves. The resulting struggle would need constant reliefs to avoid getting too tired and losing concentration and receiving sharp rebukes from the bridge.

Being Chief Quartermaster had its downsides for 'Q.M.'s worked a 24 hour watch system, 24 on and 24 off. The problems would be that when we were on official visits, or whenever H.M. the Queen wanted to go ashore, a full piping party would be required to pipe her ashore and when she returned. That meant that as I was responsible for organising these events, I had to drag at least four of the offwatch 'Q.M.s' from their slumbers to get dressed in their best uniforms. They joined all the officers and interested parties to man the Royal's gangway to play our bosun's pipe salute as H.M. left and returned. This could happen two or three times a day. So you see the 'Q.M.'s were not happy bunnies at times, and would make their feelings known towards me in no uncertain manner, 'oh well'.

There were so many stories to tell of the happenings during the times we were manning the gangways while alongside in harbour that it would need a whole biography of its own to describe them so I will depict just a few to make you smile.

The first one concerns the young sublieutenants that were serving on board. These were recently trained naval officers, university types, brash and full of themselves - quite rightly so. They had qualified for a very difficult and exacting career but when they were the Officer of the Day, they would strut out to the gangway, pretending they were swinging a cricket bat, or a tennis racquet. On one occasion one of them picked up the First Lieutenant's telescope, and as he swung it in an upwards motion it hit the girder above his head and shattered the optics, for it had telescoped outward making it longer. He stood transfixed as it dawned on him what he had done. We on the gangway, on the other hand rolled about with laughter, and asked him would he like us to tell the First Lieutenant or just leave it to him.

On another occasion, while on a visit to Bermuda I was once again on duty on the gangway, with a very surly Officer of the Day. The officer Lt. South, was surly because the yacht officers had been invited to a very special dinner party, and he had drawn the short straw by being the Officer of the Day and unable to attend the function. He made an appearance during the evening and informed me that I was to keep a special eye on the side party dinghy that was tied up in a stupid place, in between the ship and the jetty and he was afraid the ship's movement would tip the dinghy and sink it. The side party dinghy was incidentally a small boat used for going around the ship's sides touching up the paintwork and other maintenance jobs, covered in paint and dirt, it looked a poor old thing but invaluable. After he told me to look at it at intervals, I promptly forgot all about it! So when he appeared later on in the evening and peered over the side, he shouted 'Where is the damned dinghy?' The worst had happened, it had been tipped, and all you could see was the top edge just above the water. He took charge and organised buckets to be found. 'Come on you' he said to me, 'Let's bail this thing out and get it afloat again.' Fair play to him, he and I removed our socks and shoes, and managed to get into the half sunken boat and started bailing but as we nearly succeeded in our task the officers started to arrive back from their dinner date. Being merry from the tipple consumed they raised a great laugh on seeing Lt. South and myself barefoot in the dinghy. 'Are you having a nice paddle Mr. South?' they asked. They thought it was hilarious, and no doubt the subject of many social evenings in the officers mess. All I know is that from that moment on, he hated my guts, I cannot say that I blamed him, for I must have made a big dent in his ego having exposed him to the merciless humour of his fellow officers. I must say that he did go a bit too far sometimes in making life difficult for me at every opportune moment.

The job of being Quartermaster had its rewards in personal pride such as going through the ceremony of 'piping' H.M. the Queen and other 'V.I.P.s' on and off the yacht. On one occasion I had an embarrassing moment while piping H.M. the Queen ashore, for a piece of fluff had jammed itself in the pea end of my 'bosun's pipe', preventing any sound whatever being produced making a three man piping team sound very flat! If H.M. the Queen noticed she never showed any sign in the way of a grimace.

To bring an end to my Chief Quartermaster's tales was the daddy of them all. Whilst in Trinidad. I had the middle watch, midnight until 4 o'clock when much to my surprise four ambulances arrived on the quayside. I quickly despatched my bosun's mate to wake the Officer of the Day for it looked like a disaster was about to unfold.

The story was that all the lads were enjoying themselves in a friendly bar. They were led to believe that, for at one end of the bar, there was a large painting on the wall of a white hand and a black hand clasped in a friendly handshake. Things went wrong when 'Geordie' Metcalfe being the gentle creature he was tripped up on someone's foot and put his elbow through the skin of the drum that was being played on the stage. He turned around to remonstrate with the clumsy foot owner, and the irate

114

drum player hit him with a bottle! Well it was all hands to the pumps after that, the whole place erupted and the friendly handshake on the wall was forgotten.

Geordie came up the gangway first, sporting a large bandage on the side of his head, followed closely by Frank Coupland who had the whole top of his head bandaged. Geordie turned to him and said; 'When you see a cowboy film, and someone gets hit over the head with a chair, they get up and start fighting again. You Frank, you lazy bastard you just laid there!' The Surgeon Commander and his sick bay staff were summoned to double check the treatment they had all received ashore, and there were quite a few involved. The men were later dealt with by the Captain, and the bar was permanently put out of bounds to the crew.

1958 ended rather quietly, after visiting some interesting places for different royal appointments; Scilly Isles, and the Royal Naval College of Dartmouth. This was followed by our usual Cowes Regatta Week and then a very extended tour of the Western Isles of Scotland including Loch Ryan, Dunoon, Rothesay, Kilchattan, Campbeltown, Loch Tarbert, Jura, Applecross Bay and finally Fort William.

This is where I witnessed the very young Princess Anne misbehave while waiting on the gangway for the return of H.M. The Queen and the Duke of Edinburgh. The whole entourage were gathered at the gangway including Anne and Charles, Vice Admiral Connolly Able Smith, who incidentally was the Queen's uncle. We could hear the wailing of the bagpipes as H.M. the Queen left the jetty in the Royal Barge. This seemed to excite Princess Anne, who started to jump up and down, shouting 'Home Rule for Scotland' over and over again. She was sharply rebuked by Sir Connolly; 'Anne! Be quiet now'. I am sure that in her young age, she had heard it discussed many times, and thought it was the right thing to say.

Sadly this was the last year that Sir Connolly was to serve as 'F.O.R.Y.', Flag Officer Royal Yachts, as he was handing over the reins to Vice Admiral Sir Peter Dawnay. There were a succession of Admirals during the yacht's lifetime so it was strange that years later, while working for Garrards the Crown jewellers I was assisting John Garnier the clock expert and purchaser and he told me that Rear Admiral Sir John Garnier, one of the F.O.R.Y.'s was his cousin.

When Pat and I attended the paying off ceremony in 1997 I was introduced to Sir John and we had a few laughs at the antics of his eccentric cousin at Garrards who would dash around the antique venues on his motor bike buying rare clocks in different states of repair. I would then be despatched to collect the same as he could not accommodate them on his ancient machine.

So 1958 ended quietly at the end of August; earlier in the year than normal but we did not know then that 1959 was to be the year of another grand circumnavigation of the world.

Second Circumnavigation

The last four months of 1958 were taken up by the organisation and the victualling of the yacht. Once again the freshwater tanks were given over for the storing of plentiful supplies of canned beer. Who needs water when you have beer? Hundreds of spares were stored, for it would not do for the yacht to be stranded in a foreign country for the want of a spare part.

We left Portsmouth on Wednesday morning the 7th January1959 much to the dismay of our wives at the thought of such a long parting. But there you are, that was life in the Navy and had to be suffered. The wives or at least some of them were on the last jetty Sally Port to see us off as well as the B.B.C. and the Royal Marine Band. It was a horrible grey day and not very inspiring for the beginning of a world tour. The reason for the tour was to take H.R.H. Duke of Edinburgh, on a mission of flag showing and State visits that were a great asset to Britain.

It saddens me now when I think of how the Labour government was ill advised to de-commission the 'Britannia', possibly on a politically correct basis. The present generation will never experience the feeling of pride and joy of seeing the Royal Yacht, with its members of the Royal Family being welcomed in different countries. It is a fact, that wherever we went the welcome was always overwhelming. I never got used to the enthusiasm and excitement shown by the local people on our arrival. There is absolutely no doubt that these trips did immense good in cementing relations with other countries in trade and not to say the least in gaining respect for England. I am convinced that it is something that we desperately need now in a vain attempt to regain our national pride.

The first night out the crew were very quiet; this usually happened, as they were being a little nostalgic and the weather was inclement making the yacht roll and pitch. It would take a little bit of time to get their sea legs back again after such a long spell in harbour, but it would not take long for the mood to change once we started to get a bit of decent sunshine to lighten our spirits.

The first leg of our tour was by way of the Bay of Biscay to Gibraltar for a short stay to take on fuel and water. The following day saw us on the the Mediterranean to Malta, after which we were to make our way through the Suez Canal. This was the first time I had been through the canal since the days I had been there trying to stop the Egyptians from stealing it away from France and England, who were of course the original builders and owners of the project. Much to my surprise, they seemed to have made quite a good job of it. All this movement was to enable the yacht to be at Rangoon to embark H.R.H. who would have completed an extensive tour of India and Pakistan.

After an uneventful passage through the canal, we reached Aden. This would be the first time that I had ever been to Aden so I was curious to get ashore and see for myself. The British army had complete control of the place at that time so the first place I visited was the 'British' country club for a swim and drinks. After that, a couple of 'oppos' and I took a taxi ride up to Crater City where there were many shops and bazaars, so we were informed. The taxi driver refused to take any money, saying that we could pay on the return journey. When we asked what made him feel he could trust us, he gestured to the large Arab standing behind us saying that our guide would make sure we contacted him again. I am sure he would, for he stuck to us like glue until we were ready to make the return journey! I, like many others on board, was not impressed at all by Aden that was in the throes of freeing itself from the yoke of colonialism, and I think everyone was glad when we left.

The next leg was to take us through the Indian Ocean, to the Indian naval base of Vishakhapatnam where we stayed for ten days to carry out minor repairs and really get the yacht looking her best in preparation for the trip across to Rangoon and the eventual arrival of H.R.H. Duke of Edinburgh, to start his world cruise.

Vishakhapatnam was an eye opener for all of us as the amount of sad Third World deprivation that was obvious took us all by surprise. I was shocked by the sight of people crouching in the monsoon ditches alongside the road into the town carrying out their bodily functions. The poverty was everywhere. I think that as the place was an Indian naval base it led us to believe their situation would have been better.

Having pointed out the downside of 'Vishak' I feel that I must point out its assets too. It was obvious that the population was over the moon to have us there, and made that clear with the friendliness and invitations to all kind of functions. One of these was the local dancehall where we were surprised to see that the format was for the men to stand in the middle of the dance floor waiting for the young ladies to ask them to dance. We tried it but found no enthusiasm for that routine. It was amusing to see a jukebox sheltering under a thatched roof structure, installed in the village square and strange to see cows wandering in and out of their houses, as the cow is a revered animal and allowed to go where it likes. At the same time other visitors would have to remove their shoes before they entered!

There was a scheme for some of the lads to spend some time at a holiday spot at Araku, which was in a valley 70 miles from 'Vishak'. I did not go myself, but apparently it was a great success with them all. The reason I never went, was that I had been given another job change, and found myself back in the laundry.

This time I was second in charge next to P.O. 'Jan' Mayes. I say in charge, but everyone that worked there did not need any regulating as they knew exactly what they had to do and did it very well. My main functions were to be handing out the finished laundry to our customers and to balance the books with the monies collected for the same. After each session of book balancing I would take the money to Jan, who would always seem to be residing in the P.O.'s bar that was decorated with a large neon sign 'The Virg-inn', where he would take charge of the cash and then cordially invite me to have a drink, invariably I would leave sometime later a bit worse for wear. This happened too many times, so I had to time the handover when the bar was closed! When Jan left the navy, he became a publican!

One of the other features in the P.O.'s bar was a very old, but lovely Chesterfield settee in brown leather that had been the property of Queen Victoria on board her Royal Yacht 'Victoria & Albert.' I had the dubious honour of retrieving it and installing it on 'Britannia' after a working party, including myself, was sent to the lay-apart stores at Portsmouth dockyard. The store was a veritable Alladin's cave of bygone Royal Yachts. The settee lived a comfortable life in the P.O.'s bar, until they tired of it. I learned later it had a burial at sea somewhere in the Indian Ocean.

On the 14th February 1959, we left 'Vishak' for an 820 mile journey across the Bay of Bengal to Rangoon. The day before we left, the Admiral of the Fleet, Lord Fraser of North Cape, had joined us. Also included to travel with us were Miss Stevenson, a veteran of the first world cruise, and Miss Vaughan Hudson on her first trip. Both to act as secretaries to H.R.H. the Duke of Edinburgh.

The yacht was now under the command of Vice Admiral Peter Dawnay having taken over from Sir Connolly Able Smith, a great old chap. Our stay in Rangoon was to be for 24 hours, just long enough to go ashore which I and a lot of others did. Although it was interesting, I was not impressed. If we had been able to see a lot more of it, things may have been different. My impression was of a very old and used city, where as usual the poor had the worst of the deal. It has always been like that, and they have always accepted it. After I had bought a shoulder bag, decorated in typical Burmese embroidered patterns and colours, and a couple of what turned out to be quite useless bibs and bobs, I decided it was time to return to the yacht. I made my way back to the jetty to catch a boat.

To my surprise, the Admiral of the Fleet Lord Fraser was already there waiting for a liberty boat for the same reason. He turned out to be a very amiable man, who engaged me in conversation. At one point informing me that his great grandfather had been one of the former founders of the city of Rangoon. He was a man with a great deal of experience of life, and soon knew my name and how I came to be serving on the yacht. By this time a few of the officers had arrived on the jetty, and seemed curious at seeing the Admiral and I in deep conversation.

All too soon the officers' liberty boat arrived, the Admiral boarded followed closely by the other officers. I stood back out of the way as it was the officers' transport. The Admiral called out 'Come along Saxby, climb aboard' I was only too pleased to comply. He continued the conversation divided between the officers and myself all the way back to the yacht. I was now pleased with myself as I had been in personal contact with two great men; Earl Mountbatten and Lord Fraser. The next day H.R.H. the Duke of Edinburgh joined the yacht with his entourage and we sailed immediately for Singapore, and the start of the trip proper!

Our trip to Singapore was uneventful weatherwise. We had now added escorts to our number, H.M.S. Cheviot and H.M.S. Cavalier. It's strange how things turn out, for H.M.S. Cavalier is now a museum piece in its own right, installed at Chatham Dockyard. Furthermore; H.M.S. Cheviot, was the previous ship that Ernie, Pat's former boyfriend served in!

Our arrival in Singapore was quite noisy, with the army firing off a gun salute. This was the first time I had ever been to the Far East. I must say that I and many others were much impressed with the city. The cleanliness was admirable and the buildings very modern. The stay was to be for only three days which reduced the time to get to know the place. We did however get to know the China Fleet Club where the fun time came during the evening's heavy drinking. A tradition of all there, army and navy is while sitting at the long tables was to start thumping the table in unison, making all the empty glasses move along and eventually fall off the end leaving a heap of broken glass on the floor and the staff would be running around like demented beings trying to catch them to limit the damage.

One of the other products of Singapore that I remember to this day is Tiger Balm. A fiery substance that comes in small jars, that is purported to cure a hell of a lot of things. Once applied to the aching part it feels like your skin is on fire but it does seem to work. The shops were staggering, the jewellery, the clothes and knick-knacks seemed to be never ending, and reasonably priced. I only wished that I had more money at the time.

We left Singapore on the 25th February to a tumultuous send off by masses of people. Small boats and a wonderful display by fire fighting boats spraying coloured water into the air as a salute. This was the stuff royal visits were made of. We appreciated it, and they enjoyed doing it. How very different today where hate and indifference seems to be the norm.

The next leg of our journey was Borneo, we were to sail to the Kuching River and proceed several miles up it to a village called Tanjong Sadap where H.R.H. was due to disembark to tour Sarawak and North Borneo by land and air. We were greeted at the village by boats dressed as dragons,

The hardworking laundry crew

and water skiers carrying a banner with, 'Welcome Prince Philip' clearly displayed. The village was completely surrounded by dense jungle. A weird feeling to be on a ship so close to the vegetation.

To remind ourselves, just in case we are losing the thread, I would like to draw the reader's eye to the fact, that all this time yours truly was sweating away below decks in the laundry doing my bit to keep the ships company, and the Royal staff, clean and presentable.

The funny cartoon, was produced by a very talented amateur artist by the name of 'Darkie' Thomas, who was a member of the Royal Marine Band. I think it was quite well observed and captured the moment in 120 degrees of heat. The constant supply of cans of beer was absolutely essential! I had the job of taking care of the Duke's shirts. As he refused to have any starch in his clothes, ironing the shirts became a nightmare, with the super softness of the material, and sometimes looking worse on completion than when I had started.

My other duties were to operate the starching machine that heavily starched and polished the stiff fronted shirts and winged collars for the officers dress attire. You had to be careful with the winged collars, and not make the edges at all rough, which could result in slitting their throats! All this along with collecting the money for the laundry made me a busy boy. Darkie went on to produce a number of appropriate cartoons during the cruise dealing with different occasions.

We sailed the very next morning on the 27th February, up the west coast of Borneo for our new destination of Sandakan. Our stay was to be a little longer this time; 1st to the 3rd March as H.R.H. was intending to join us there on completion of his tour of the country. Sandakan was a busy commercial town that had been mistreated by the Japanese during its occupation, decimating the buildings and population. Now it boasted many new buildings, and a thriving business in hardwoods. The population was made up of Chinese, Dyaks, Indians and Malays. I know that this was a time before the emergence of computers, but it was strange to see the Chinese shopkeepers adding up the takings on the abacus.

The days spent at Sandakan while waiting were well spent in ways of sport, tourism and log rolling. Yes it's true, but the 'yachties' failed miserably at that. Needless to say, I did not partake in any of that. The fact is that I must be a terribly wimpy guy that is not fond of sports at all.

The log rolling bit turned out hilarious at one point, for hundreds of spectators gathered on the end of the wooden jetty to observe the competition, the weight of which made the wooden jetty sink slowly but surely into the mud.. On the other hand, the 'yachties' did very well at football and cricket, played out in the very fine stadium. The last big event was an open-air dance, 'din-dang', where the dance partners weave about in front of each other without actually touching, this lasted eight hours! Our lads tried it, but in comparison to the native people, they looked rather inelegant. Especially the ones who'd had a drink or two. Never mind, the exercise did them all a bit of good, for we hadn't been on shore leave since leaving Vishakapatnam.

On the 3rd March we left Sandakan on a three day journey to Hong Kong. Our passage took us by the way of the Sulu Sea and the Lanakapan Straits to the China Sea.. We arrived at Hong Kong on the 6th March safe and sound with the exception of a near collision with a merchant ship, who only obeyed the rule of the road, after 'Britannia' gave a blast on her siren.

The reception we received was ecstatic with fire crackers, ships sirens, gun salutes and of course the crowds of people. After securing to a buoy in the harbour the visiting boats came crowding around controlled by the Hong Kong police. One such boat was Jennie's side boat. These side party boats were employed by the Royal Navy to work on the naval ship sides, painting and washing, keeping them in tip top condition.

The main difference with Jennie's boat from the many others that plied for work, was that she only employed girl workers! When Prince Philip was a serving naval officer Jennie was his choice for any of the ships he served on. So it was that she was allowed alongside that day, to be greeted like an old friend, and to deliver a present in the shape of a beautifully carved Camphor Wood Chest for Prince Philip.

The next job to be done, was to erect the huge, white waxed awning over the sun deck, which was done with the help of all available seaman. First the awning had to be brought up from the stowage. It came up from the after hatch in the form of a sixty foot long trussed up sausage, which was then draped over the central steel hawser that ran the entire length of the sun deck tent fashion, and then spread out either side to the upright stanchions that remained in position always. Once all the relevant fixing eyes were attached to the stanchions, it was tightened up to form a nicely shaded deck that would be used for receptions and cocktail parties to honour the local V.I.P.s.

The sun deck had a glass fronted lounge in front of which stood the ornate compass. If you can picture in your mind this area after its early morning clean, decks scrubbed, brasses all polished, everything fresh and white, if you can imagine it, then you have captured the essence of the navy.

As this was the first visit to Hong Kong for a lot of us, we were eager to get ashore to sample the aura of H.K. that we had heard so much about from older hands used to serving in the Far East. It turned out to be just as they had described it, even down to the fact that you could be measured for a suit, and receive the finished article 24 hours later. One could almost imagine the tailors sitting crossed legged on a table sewing and stitching all night long.

The whole town was bathed in bright lights to entice people into the fabulous shops. Once again you could not help but notice the strange clicking and banging noises that seemed to come from every dwelling. This time it was not the abacus but mahjong, the game played with ivory blocks in a format that was supposed to represent the Great Wall of China.

All too soon our small supply of money ran out, and a sailor without money is about as welcome to the locals as a blow on the head! We were not very well paid in the services in those days, so after purchasing a few toys for the kids, and having a few obligatory drinks, it was back on board to get ready for the next leg of the cruise, the South Sea Islands.

The departure from H.K. was noisy and eventful in as much as one of our escort ships, the New Zealand Navy ship, 'Rotoiti' accidentally sank a sampan in a collision with it during its manoeuvre on leaving the harbour. Fortunately no one was hurt.

Our cruise to the islands was to take up nearly a month, we were to make seven landfalls; Gizo, Honiara, Malaita, Graciosa Bay, Tarawa, Ocean Island, Vaitupu and Christmas Island. That particular part of the cruise would cover 7,643 nautical miles but the first hurdle was the ten day journey to the first island Gizo in the Solomon Islands, but as we passed through the Bismarck Archipelago, H.R.H. decided he would like to have a ban yan on Tench Island.

Now this little speck of land, only one mile long and three quarters of a mile wide, stood up like a pimple in thousands of miles of ocean, was amazingly inhabited. The yacht anchored off, and the islanders came out in their outrigger canoes, to ferry people ashore over the dangerous coral reef. Tench Island turned out to be a wonderful place, with the friendly people living a blameless life, fishing, fishing, and even more fishing. It would prove to be very boring for the likes of us, but there, we had been spoilt by our modern way of living. Nevertheless, they were very happy, and I envy them for their piece of heaven, but would remain for ever nervous of living on a small speck of land like that.

After the Duke had enjoyed some sailing in 'Cowslip', his own private yacht, that was carried on the boat deck for his use, we upped anchor and slipped away from Tench, and immediately started to get ready for the 'crossing the line ceremony'. This would be for initiating the ships members who had not crossed the line before. I myself had been through the ceremony while on the previous world

Villagers at Malaita, Solomon Islands

trip. On crossing the equator the imaginary line around the world, one has to come to terms with King Neptune, by being suspended above a swimming pool, in a tippable chair, you are soaped and shaved with a giant wooden razor by Neptune's aids. After which you are further humiliated by continued ducking. For this you receive a scroll declaring that you are now one of Neptune's subjects. Silly really but quite a lot of fun, especially on a long boring sea voyage between landfalls.

On the 18th March the yacht arrived off Gizo in the Solomon Islands. Two war canoes came out to meet us, they looked quite ferocious, but then when one looked closely items of modern clothing could be seen which took the edge off the illusion just a little. 'Britannia' picked her way through the coral reef along a channel marked by coloured buoys, previously laid by the Royal Navy survey ship H.M.S. Cook. This system was to be repeated throughout our Pacific trip for it would not be appropriate for the Royal Yacht to finish up on a far flung coral reef.

The stay at Gizo was not to be for long as we were due to arrive at our next port of call Honiara the next day, the19th. The stay was long enough for H.R.H. to be taken ashore, feted with garlands around his neck by grass skirted females, I think he loved it all. We sailed in the afternoon and arrived at Honiara the next morning.

Honiara is a town that is steeped in history as far as World War II is concerned. It is the biggest town in the Guadalcanal, and the struggle between the Japanese and the Americans is so hugely documented, that there is no need to dwell on that subject. There was plenty of evidence in the form of rusting Japanese ships and military equipment laying on the beaches, to remind us of what happened in those days gone by. Once again we sailed that day bound for Malaita.

Early next morning the 20th, found us once again picking our way through a particularly nasty piece of coral reef at the entrance to Malaita. But thanks to the endeavours of H.M.S. Cook our safety had been ensured. We were amazed to see one of our support vessels 'Coral Queen' that was carrying the transport car for the use of H.R.H. was hard and fast on the coral reef. No one seemed to know how she managed to get there seeing that a channel had been clearly marked out. We could only conclude that as she was a resident boat, a lot of overconfidence was to blame for her undoing.

Malaita had a reputation for having some of the most violent hill tribesmen in the Solomon Islands. In fact thirty years before our visit, two government officials and their entire police guard were slaughtered while trying to collect taxes from them, so there was a little bit of apprehension when I and two of my 'oppos' managed to step ashore. This was heightened by the fact that we came across these tribesmen soon after setting foot on dry land. The men seemed to be very tall with painted bodies, and smelling none too pleasant, but they seemed amiable enough when offered a few cigarettes. I was only too glad they didn't suspect us of trying to collect any taxes!

During our meandering of the island we accidentally managed to wander into the official ceremony of welcome by the island population to H.R.H. Nobody seemed to mind so we stayed and

Oh those dancing feet, you could just not stop them

watched him being given the fragrant frangipani garlands after which we found ourselves being engaged in conversation by the natives who were keen to show us their skills in climbing the coconut palms and collected a few for us to take back on board. The funny thing was they talked us into buying one of the thatched huts for forty cigarettes. For a while the three of us sat in our property laughing and joking with all these people until it was time to return on board. Realising we could not take our property with us they promised to look after it until we returned. I wonder if it is still there, or if we still own it!

At 6 o'clock we sailed down the coast to Auki, this being the capital of Malaita. The Duke re-embarked before setting sail for Graciosa Bay. The 22nd March found us anchoring off Graciosa Bay, the last island of the Solomon's group. The welcoming arrangements included the decorating of the villages, and we were greeted by the large smiles and excitement of the villagers, also we were intrigued by the appearance of the tribal hillsmen armed with spears and bows and poison tipped arrows! Naturally we had no desire to find out if this was true or not. We were assured that these implements were only used for hunting, but for what? A very pleasant day observing their lifestyle, and I am sure a pleasant day for them, as they do not have a member of Royalty dropping in every day.

We sailed at 5pm for Tarawa which was to be the first island in the Gilbert and Ellis group. It may seem that we quit the islands in some undue haste, but when you consider the very large distances between them, it was necessary not to stay too long otherwise the trip could not be completed on time! Anyway, to have stayed longer may have resulted in us wearing out our welcome. Captain Cook did just that, and you know what happened to him!

Another three days at sea and we reached Tarawa where H.M.N.Z.S. 'Rotoiti' and ourselves dropped anchors well outside the coral reefs. It looked as if we had to rely on the local boats for transport ashore. These islands were remarkable, for they were actually formed of the present living and the dead coral over millions of years. There is no denying the complexity of the forces of nature. There were two small islands in this atoll, Bairiki and Betio, the latter being the busier commercial place of the two. It was originally obliterated by the Americans during their landings when trying to shift the Japanese.

There followed the usual goodwill gestures on both sides, our side seemed to have captured the heart and the mood of these occasions, for they performed well in enthusiastically taking up all challenges to sporting activities. Sometimes being disappointed in the results, as was the case at Tarawa, when the barefooted opposing team thrashed them at cricket. There was dancing by the native population, who gloried in it, and did it at any possible excuse.

There was one incident that took place there, when one of the lads while fishing over the ship's side, a very popular pastime, hooked a shark! After realising they were unable to get it up the ship's side and over the gunwale without someone getting bitten a boat was detached and the shark shot through the head while at water level. The line broke and it got away.

While all this shark baiting was taking place I was in my workplace i.e. the laundry. I heard all the banging and thumping on the ship's side and opened the porthole to see what was going on, and promptly came face to face with a struggling, snapping seven foot shark being hauled up the ship's side by a shouting crowd of lunatics above. On reflection they realised they could not safely haul it over the ship's handrail, so they lowered it down into the water again, thus giving me a second look down its throat as it passed by. I dread to think what the outcome may have been if they had managed to land it the first time. As I mentioned previously it was shot, and then managed to break loose. The strange part was that some three hours later, they hooked another shark that did not put up the same resistance, and when they did finally haul it aboard, to everyone's amazement it turned out to be the same shark, borne out by the bullet holes in its head. This time it was in a dying state but still able to go for bait. I know all this sounds a bit far-fetched, but I assure you it was perfectly true. We had been at Tarawa for two days, but now it was time to leave for Ocean Island; two days journey this time.

Ocean Island came as a big surprise to us, and partially eclipsed our romantic image of the South Sea Islands. For civilisation had caught up here, as Ocean Island being volcanically formed had large deposits of phosphates. One half was covered in industrial machines and processing plants, destroying any natural beauty that was there. The other half looked to be untouched, but I am sure that would not last.

It was revealed that during the Japanese occupation, every inhabitant was shot, bar one who managed to escape and tell the tale. It was without regret that our stay was to be only for the day when we sailed once again, this time for what turned out to be a very pleasant place, thus restoring our expectations. Vaitupu, could only be described as a gem of a place. The moment we arrived the yacht was met and surrounded by native canoes and boats, all singing and beating the sides of their craft with their oars, in perfect rhythm with their song of welcome. H.R.H. the Duke, was transported to the shore in one of the war canoes.

On reaching the shore the canoe was hoisted shoulder high by what must have been very strong young men, with H.R.H. and his companion still sitting in it, and were carried up to the village. After the dancing and singing and welcoming speeches a massive feast had been prepared for the important guests, who were seated opposite a beautiful girl, whose only purpose was to regulate the diners meal, by signalling to the waiting bodies that the next part of the meal should be served.

Apparently when the important diner could eat no more of any part of the meal, it was passed back to the non-important guests! I am glad to say that none of us were considered for either position, 'just onlookers'. The menu consisted of; suckling pig, breadfruit, coconut and other fruits. All eaten off palm leaves while seated on the ground. All in all it was reminiscent of what must have taken place in

H.R.H. the Duke of Edinburgh being carried shoulder high in the canoe

those far off days of Mutiny on the Bounty, and Captain Cook. Having been privileged to witness such splendid sights, it was with a pang of sadness that we sailed at 6.30pm for the last island of our trip; Christmas Island.

I think most people know that Christmas Island was the base for Britain's atomic testing sites in the Pacific, so it was not a big surprise to find that the whole island was occupied by the combined

Enjoying the celebrations at Vaitupu

Services, and imported labour from the surrounding islands. Although the native workers were not indigenous to Christmas Island, they had certainly brought their customs with them, and treated us to an exhibition of hula dancing, grass skirts and all. Once again, our cricket team was thrashed by a barefoot team of seemingly experts, and the football team was thrashed by the resident combined Services opposition. The weather suddenly turned foul, and we spent some of the time sheltering from

Gilbertese children putting on a good display

the ferocious rainstorms. Our two day visit was soon up and we prepared to sail on the 5th April this time our nose would be pointed the way home by way of the Panama Canal which in any event was a surprising fourteen day trip away.

The fourteen day journey across the Pacific was long, and would have been arduous except for the upper deck sports that took place between the departments. One such event was 'deck hockey', when played in the confines of the deck space that we had, became a very contact sport indeed. The series was won by the Royal Household staff, led by Prince Philip, who did not escape without his fair share of injuries from the flying hockey sticks!

Other contests included chess and 'uckers', this being the modified method of playing ludo that was adopted by the navy. A much more exciting way that managed to stir up agitation among the four players taking part, demanding tactical skills plus a good deal of optimism.

The weather was not too kind to us, and the rain increased as we drew nearer to Balboa, and the Panama Canal. I have recently watched a research programme on the Panama Canal, and was amazed at the number of people who were killed or died of various diseases during the twenty odd years it took before the canal was completed. Started by the French, then abandoned after the monsoon like rains kept washing the soil back into the digging. The job was taken up by the Americans under President Roosevelt, with the intention of allowing the Americans easy access to the Pacific. After a good deal of troubled working, and a great deal of money the job was finished, and is truly one of the great wonders of the world, connecting the Pacific and the Atlantic via a series of locks to take you up to a great man made lake, and then more locks to take you down.

The yacht was manoeuvred into our berth at Balboa by Prince Philip, quite skilfully. He was by now very fond of 'Britannia', and loved being in charge of handling her. I was reliably informed that during the cruise he would appear on the bridge while the yacht was at sea and take up position in the Admiral's high seat and blend in with the organisation going on there. On one occasion the young signalman was ordered to go down to the galley to make a warming pot of cocoa, 'ki'. This being the navy special drink at sea, made from what looks like a large bar of chocolate, that has to be scraped off into small flakes and then boiled to produce a thick chocolate drink, it also contains arrowroot. When you wrapped yourself around a cup of that on cold wet nights on the bridge it would sustain one very much. The signalman saluted and asked Prince Philip if he would like a cup of 'ki' and was shocked when the Duke replied 'no thank you yeoman, 'ki' makes me fart like a Trojan!'. H.R.H. was always a man's man, and his forthright manner of speaking was to earn him some criticism as would be demonstrated in future times.

Our arrival at Balboa was to be overshadowed by fear of an insurrection of Panama, in the form of a seaborne invasion by the would be leader Robert Arias, who surprisingly was married to our own Dame Margot Fonteyn, at that time England's prima ballerina. Anyway nothing happened whilst we were there, thus sparing us a very embarrassing situation.

133

Our transition through the canal was both smooth and very interesting, and filled us with admiration at the way the traction engines 'mules' towed us along to the points required. Once we had risen to the lakes, which we traversed under our own power, we were to repeat the locks, only this time downward and into the colon which is at the other end of the canal. The next day we sailed for Nassau in the Bahamas, some two hundred and fifty miles off the coast of Miami. H.R.H. was due to leave us there to fly back to the U.K.

We arrived at Nassau on the 24th April and was due to stay for two days. Although Nassau is a British controlled island, it is at the same time completely influenced by the American tourist trade, and so prices were pretty high. This would put a financial strain on the crew's ability to enjoy the island. As it turned out, there was no need to worry for local people were only too willing to entertain us all.

My own experience of this happened when my 'oppo' Arthur Crane and I stepped ashore after being invited to the American's Wives League Dance. Having found the venue, we were welcomed and given three tickets for three free drinks. On ordering our first one, the barman filled the half pint glass three-quarters full with Rum and put a dash of Coca Cola on the top. Something told me that we would not need very many of the tickets! The dance itself went very well, and the Americans proved to be great conversationalists who seemed to be obsessed with royalty. I can only assume that they miss not being included in the family; they only have themselves to blame!

The dance ended and the group of people that we were with announced that they intended to go on to an open air nightclub, and that we were not to worry about the cost, for we were their guests.

The nightclub turned out to be a truly exotic place with subdued lights and the whole place surrounded by palm trees that lent a nice picturesque view on that balmy night. Arthur and I got down to a plentiful supply of drinks with stimulating banter going on among the tables around us. There was a roll of drums and the Master of Ceremonies announced that they often had celebrities visit their club and that tonight they were honoured to have Pat Boone in the audience.

The spotlight shone on the appropriate table and Mr. Boone stood up to the claps and cheers for the well known singer. Unfortunately Arthur also stood up and blew a very loud raspberry in Mr. Boone's direction. I must add that he was by this time a little worse for wear due to the amount of rum and coke he had consumed. Well there is hardly any need to tell you that the proprietors were not too pleased and promptly ejected us, Arthur and myself that is. When I angrily asked him why he did it, he simply said that he didn't like Pat Boone, although I wasn't too happy at the time having had a very pleasant evening cut short, we always have a good laugh now and again at our annual get together.

Arthur was a happy go lucky sort of person, who always seemed nearer to laughter than any other sort of emotion. It wasn't the first time we had been in trouble in the nightclub scene. When he and I were ashore in Oslo, some time before, we became involved with a group of people drinking in a bar, who consequently invited us along with them to the nightclub they had chosen to visit, 'Their treat'.

Things went very well and everyone was enjoying themselves, the music was good, and the entertainment on the stage was excellent. All too soon we were becoming slightly intoxicated. A meal was ordered and this turned out to be in the form of one whole cooked chicken each, which was accompanied by a huge finger bowl placed in the centre of the table. That's where the trouble started. The person sitting opposite Arthur thought it was funny to throw his chicken bones into the finger bowl thus splashing him with water each time. Arthur growled to me 'If he does that one more time, I'm going to put his lights out'. My protests to him not to spoil the situation by a hasty decision was cut short by the offending gent throwing the remainder of his chicken into the bowl, thus covering Arthur in water who in turn promptly jumped up and hit the offending person between the eyes, laying him out in his chair.

Of course the persons that were to be ejected from the club were going to be us as the other side were paying the bills. It is still vivid in my memory that as they surrounded Arthur, he was reaching for his chicken in a vain hope of taking it with him.

He left the Royal Yacht Service before I did, and I learned years later that he became a 'Master at Arms' after working his way up through the regulating branch of the service. Naval Police; now isn't that a turn up for the books? When I showed surprise at this revelation, bearing in mind his past exploits, he simply said 'If you can't beat them Chas. join them'.

We left Nassau on the 26th April, and after a short stop at Bermuda for fuel our journey was continued onto the U.K. arriving home at Portsmouth on the 7th May. The cruise had been a great success with the organisation running as smooth as silk, with one or two exceptions. One of these being the difficulty we managed to get ourselves into on our last stop at Bermuda, for as we attempted to leave for our last leg of the cruise we found that the current was holding us firmly onto the jetty. It was finally decided to attach ourselves to a buoy out in the harbour by means of a steel cable and pull ourselves off the jetty. After a lot of heaving on the capstans, 'winches', it was realised that we were not moving at all, but the buoy had moved a lot nearer to us. That idea was abandoned, and the buoy released, which immediately streaked back to its original position like a speed boat, nearly colliding with one of the small boats in the harbour. In the end a tug had to be summoned to assist us!

Our arrival at Portsmouth was welcomed by the families gathered on the harbourside eagerly waiting to greet us. Our journey had taken us 170 days to complete, travelling a distance of 24,537 miles and enriched our personal experiences unbelievably. So ended an enjoyable time. We were comforted by the news that the yacht was not required until June. That would give us some time with our families.

St. Lawrence Seaway - Official Opening

Our next duty on the 6th June was to take H.M. the Queen and H.R.H to Canada for the official opening of the St. Lawrence Seaway but the first job was to spend time in the dockyard, being fitted with an elm rubbing strake down either side of the yacht just below the water line, and out of sight. These strakes were to assist us when in the locks of the new seaway, in the hope of avoiding any damage to the pristine painted blue hull. We were to experience that it would need a lot more than that to prevent damage! The other extensive modification, was the novel idea of hinging the top of the main mast, to enable us to pass underneath the iron structures. The first thing that had to be done, was to cut off twenty-one foot from the top of the main mast, this being the tallest of the three masts. The open ends were then capped by metal plates and welded over, and then hinges fitted. All this was necessary to allow us to lower the top of the mast to give us enough clearance to get through, and for some reason this was called 'scandalising'. These 'mods' needed a scaffolding to be put up around the mast. An idea formed in my mind at seeing this, for I knew the tradition was that commemorative coins were always laid in place at the bottom of the main mast of a newly built ship. Realising that the top of the mast would be open for a short while, and the mast was hollow all the way to the bottom I busied myself filing flat three pennies in 'old money' , which I then stamped with my name and relevant details on the clean flat side. Late at night I climbed the scaffolding and dropped my pennies into the open end and listened as they tinkled all the way to the bottom to join up with the commemorative coins already there, 'I hoped'. I like to think that in the future they will be discovered, and the discoverers wonder on how on earth they got there! At the time of writing they have already been there forty-seven years.

The forthcoming trip for the opening of the St. Lawrence Seaway, was to be another momentous occasion for us all including the great honour put to our Queen to perform the ceremony. The Seaway was another eighth wonder of the world, and was a project by Canada and America to cut a canal to join up the lakes Erie, Huron, Michigan, and finally Lake Superior. This would enable ships to traverse from Montreal to Chicago and beyond, to Port Arthur in Minnesota and Ontario; what an achievement!

The lakes turned out to be a surprise as they were more inland seas rather than lakes, and could get quite rough at times!.

After our very short break with our families, we left Portsmouth on the 6th June for Canada. 'Join the navy and see the world!' Prior to the trip, it was decided that I needed a job change as I was now a Leading Seaman. I was drafted into the boat party to be a boat's Coxswain, 'boat driver'. It was a period when I was to discover that boat driving was not one of the best things that I could do! Another experienced driver was allocated to me, in the role of mentor, a good 'oppo' of mine Charlie Chorlton. He and I had spent a lot of time together as Royal Barges crew in previous years.

Thinking back to those times, one humorous occasion springs to mind when we were taking Prince Philip, and Commander Mike Parker, H.R.H.'s personal aide, on a ban yan to a tropical island. As the beach area was so shallow, we towed a dinghy behind the barge which would drop anchor just off the beach in deeper waters, and ferry the Duke and his party the rest of the way with the dinghy. On this occasion, I was drawing the dinghy alongside to get it ready and Charlie was standing behind me. Without looking, I handed him the dinghy's rope saying 'here, hold this a minute', this was to allow me to jump in the dinghy and fit the rowlocks that take the oars. When I looked up H.R.H. was standing there with the rope in his hand! I found out later that Charlie had moved out of the way when H.R.H. moved down the barge's side, in anticipation of boarding the dinghy!

Charlie volunteered to row the party onto the beach, so I relaxed on the barge and watched the progress. I was amazed to see Charlie at one point jump over the side of the dinghy, and finish up to his neck in the water, and walk the dinghy in the rest of the way! I thought to myself, 'the old groveller, he's trying to impress H.R.H.'. I found out later that what transpired was that on nearing the beach, the Duke peering over the side, calculated that the water was only a couple of feet deep, and told Charlie to jump over and pull the dinghy in. Charlie protested, saying that it looked a lot deeper than that. H.R.H. insisted but on seeing Charlie up to his neck, only laughed and said, 'Well you're in now so get cracking'.

My driving instructions were to start in Portsmouth, with control and manoeuvering of the 27 ft twin engine escort boat. In my first effort I managed to clip the dockyard wall, thus doing damage to the 'A' frame bracket that carries the propeller! My period of depressing incidents had begun. It was the 6th June and we said goodbye to our loved ones, who by this time were getting used to these traumatic farewells. As a goodwill gesture, considering the importance of the occasion; two officers and fifteen ratings, plus one W.R.E.N. Petty Officer of the Royal Canadian Navy were drafted on board while we were in Portsmouth and were to remain with us for the duration of the trip. One of these, A.B.

Seaman Martin Marcotte a French Canadian rating, was drafted into my mess deck, and we immediately became good 'oppos'.

The dockyard had done us proud during our modifications by repainting the yacht's sides in a beautiful gloss, making her a lovely sight. But all in vain, for as soon as we put to sea, we ran into a force eight gale which on the Beaufort Scale, means 'nasty'. The weather stayed with us all the way across the Atlantic, mixed with thick fog, and just to liven things up, icebergs at close quarters. We finally arrived at Point Edward Naval Base at Sydney on Cape Breton. A nice surprise was to be finding a detachment of 'Mounties' waiting to greet us.

These policemen were to be living on board for the duration of the trip and manned the gangways whenever the yacht was alongside the various jetties. They were also to provide protection for the various dignitaries that were to be on board. I must say that they really looked splendid in their traditional red coats, and stetson type hats. Under no circumstances could they be persuaded to let us dress up in them for photographic purposes, even though they were living on our messdecks. Not even when they were plied with sippers of our daily rum ration, which they seemed to enjoy very much!

On the 18th June, we moved off up the St. Lawrence River, to anchor off Sept Isles to await the arrival of H.M. The Queen and Prince Philip due on the 20th. My baptism by fire was to take place here, in the form of putting my scant knowledge of boat driving to the test. The first operation I was to take part in, was to help transport the Queen's and Royal Household baggage back to 'Britannia'. All this baggage had arrived with the household in advance of the Royal Party. My boat was heavily loaded, but it was not until I was approaching the yacht's gangway ladder that I realised that the boat was responding very slowly to my steering and as a result I missed the gangway completely!

I circled to make another run at the gangway, only to find to my horror that I was to repeat my first error, and miss the gangway again, but not by such a big margin this time, 'I was improving'. As I passed, I looked up to see Lt. South, who was unfortunately for me the present officer in charge of the boat party. I could see by his expression that he was not happy. Looking back to the time in Bermuda, and the episode of the side party dinghy, I was sure that I was going to be in for a rough ride at his hands. Fortunately the third time was lucky and I succeeded in a great manoeuvre to bring the boat alongside the gangway. As I was the one to take the first boatload, the following boats benefited from my attempts, making me look like the only idiot.

My ill luck was to follow me into my first 24 hour stint as duty boat for liberty men. The yacht

139

was anchored some way out from Sept Isles, due to the shallowness of the water. This made it quite a long run into shore. The first half of our shift went well, but became more and more difficult due to a downturn in the weather. We found ourselves, the boats crew, battling through very rough waters, increasing in severity on each trip. After our last official trip, the boats falls were lowered to hoist our boat out of the water for the night, thus putting it out of harms way from the worsening weather.

Now this operation in bad circumstances can be a very nerve-racking thing, for when the 'falls' are lowered there are large heavy hooks on the end of the steel ropes that have to be put in a position where the hooks can be put through the large eye bolts on the deck of the boat. This is done by a member of the crew on each end of the boat grabbing a hook, and simultaneously locating them into the eyebolts, and signalling by holding up one arm to let me, as Coxswain, know that all was ready, at the same time, trying hard not to lose a few fingers in the jerking, jumping heavy hooks and eyes.

My part in this operation as driver was to bring the boat under the falls, and keep it there by manipulating the engines. After a few heart stopping moments due to the boat rising and falling on the waves which at one moment would take us up on their crests, then drop away, letting the boat drop, only to stop with a sickening thud at the end of the falls.

The officer in charge of the hoisting, on seeing the boat was hooked up, proceeded to bring the boat up to the top of the davits. As soon as we cleared the water, all the wild movements stopped, bringing a great sigh of relief from one and all. After securing, the crew went below to climb into our hammocks for a well earned rest until our next official trip at 8am the next morning. Wrong!

At midnight one of the Quartermaster's shook me in my hammock to inform me that the boat was required to go inshore to bring the yacht's doctor back from Sept Isles where he had been to a dinner in honour of something or other. After collecting my crew, we manned the boat, and reversing what we had done a short time earlier, we were lowered into the water, which by this time was very angry. As soon as we touched down the frenzy began. The boat started to heave about like a demon, the spray was lashing all about us, I put the engines in for'ard motion. The waves had increased in height making it only possible to see the shoreline when we rose to the crests of the waves. Some of the crew crowded into the cockpit with me, while the engineer rating remained below in his engine room, singing loudly trying to outdo the roaring of the machinery. I think he did this out of nervousness, either in fear of the weather, or the rookie Coxswain!

At one point, one of the crew stumbled in the cockpit and knocked a foam fire extinguisher from its position to fall heavily on the deck, and the damned thing went off covering the deck with slippery foam. Things were descending into a Keystone Cops comedy as I slipped and lost control of the steering wheel. The boat swung round parallel to the waves in a position that is known as broaching to, the result of which is that the boat is in danger of rolling right over. Fortunately I regained control and we finally entered the harbour and located the doctor. After a short interlude to regain our composure we set off for the return journey on having cleared up the mess left by the foam.

The brightly lit yacht was easy to see so we had no trouble there. But when arriving at the gangway ladder where the doctor had to alight, we could see the waves were at one moment about four rungs up the ladder, and the next well below. This meant he had to wait his opportunity to jump as we were falling past the ladder, and then quickly spring up to avoid getting wet and for a man who has just returned from an eating and drinking spree, he succeeded quite well.

Having deposited our passenger, I turned the boat towards the 'falls' hoping that we could get hoisted, but on the first try the boat was being tossed about so badly that one, or even both the crew were going to be injured by the hooks as they crashed about on the deck every time we were thrown upwards by the large waves that had by now developed.

The officer on the upper deck rather than risk the obvious dangers ordered me to take the boat back inshore to the safety of the harbour for the night and to keep in constant contact by our walkie-talkie. A sleepless night for me alongside the jetty, making sure the boat was not fouling on the jetty, and making sure that the locals didn't sneak any parts off the boat for mementos, all while my crew slumbered away in the main cabin.

The next morning everything had calmed down on arriving back at the yacht, we were immediately hoisted and examined by the boat officer who gleefully found a damaged 'A' frame, back to square one. Oh well, after all I was Lt. South's favourite person.

On the 20th June H.M. the Queen and Prince Philip arrived and took up residence on board. There was to be a six day gap before our arrival at Montreal where we were to be joined by President Eisenhower of the U.S.A., and Mr Diefenbaker, Prime Minister of Canada and their lady wives for the formal opening of the Seaway. Until then the Royal Family would visit a number of ports such as the quaintly named Ha Ha Bay. We spent some time in Quebec, the home town of my recently acquired 'oppo' Martin Marcotte, who insisted on taking me ashore to meet his family, who seemed only able to speak French! We had a great time, and got slightly inebriated with all the toasts that transpired, 'Vive!'.

After that we moved on to a river cruise ship that was taking hundreds of young people on a four day cruise up the Saguenay River. The whole crew seemed to be relations of Martin and they were determined to ply us with as much wine and spirit as they possibly could leaving us in a happy state.

It was only by good fortune that they didn't take us with them, for the ship was about to leave and they were actually lifting the gangway when we managed to run across it to get ashore. I am sure that our careers as Royal Yachtsmen would have been cut short that day if we had gone missing on a four day cruise, and returned as gibbering idiots, 'fun though'.

After leaving Quebec on the 24th June, we made our way to Montreal, where we were due to meet the President and the Prime Minister on the 26th for the start of the opening ceremony. It was a truly madcap journey as we were constantly surrounded by masses of small power craft eager to join the fun. How nobody was killed in the fracas still remains a mystery.

On the way down the river we passed the town of Trois Rivieres which was deeply involved with papermaking, this was obvious by the whole place being surrounded by huge piles of logs. These logs were a forewarning to all our boat drivers of the difficult time that awaited us while trying to perform our duties.

After arriving at Montreal, and securing alongside the jetty, the preparations for the big ceremony really moved into top gear, with the cleaning etc, also with the delivery of a number of very large rubber fenders, they were blown up with air, and were to be used as a protection in between the ships side and the walls of the locks. We experienced the need for them once the yacht was in the lock. This was large enough to hold two or three ships at any one time, and the water is either let in or out. The result was to push the ship up against the wall, and at the same time either drop the level or raise it, causing a drag that could be terribly damaging to the ship's side.

In practice it turned out that the water pressure was so great that the rubber fenders started to explode and sounded like guns firing making it necessary for us to use the normal rope fenders which were sometimes pulled out of our hands. We lost a lot of fenders in those bizarre circumstances.

Once again my Canadian 'oppo' Martin, managed to get my arm in a half nelson lock, and force me to accompany him ashore to meet even more of his family! It seemed that his family covered half of Canada. Once again things turned out quite convivially with some good food and drink, with Martin translating, It was strange how these French Canadians stuck doggedly to their native language in a mainly English speaking country. I'm sure they understood English quite well, but chose not to use it.

It was decided that all the family, including Martin and myself, were to go out that evening to their favourite night spot which we did. It was a very nice place with a floorshow, good music, and naturally a great deal of drink! At one point during the floorshow, the young lady who was demonstrating her ability to do the Charleston whilst twirling some red tassels fixed to the nipples of her breasts stopped abruptly and spoke in French to the audience. To which Martin jumped up and replied in French. To my surprise, everyone started to clap, and look in our direction. I asked him what was going on and he told me that the girl had asked for one of the audience to come up and assist her and that he had just volunteered me for the job, much to the amusement of his family.

But I did as I was bid, and much to my embarrassment, went through a number of routines with her to hoots of encouragement of all there. All in all a terrific evening out, and something very hard to live down as Martin made sure everyone on board the yacht knew how ridiculous I had looked up there on the stage!

The rest of our stay in Montreal proved to be a great strain on the boat drivers abilities. For as previously mentioned this was a timber production country, and that meant there was a great deal of giant rafts of logs being towed up and down the Seaway, some of which could, and did break away, leaving them bobbing up and down in the water for all the world like World War II mines, and could do shocking damage to boats in a collision.

It was necessary to travel at a cautious speed, and have one of the boat's crew perched on the bow of the boat doing his best to spot them and point a finger at the offending log, whereas we boat drivers would yank the steering over in a desperate attempt to avoid the danger.

This all worked reasonably well, except when bringing back a boatload of liberty men from ashore, who had been busy trying to get as much beer down themselves in the shortest time possible. For when on these occasions we had to perform the violent manoeuvre of the boat it would bring howls of agony from the men with trembling stomachs, and maybe even worse results. But there, being the person I am, I would laugh to myself every time I had to perform the movement, and even did it when it was not necessary!

The 26th June, saw the arrival of the President of the United States: President Eisenhower and Mr Diefenbaker, Prime Minister of Canada accompanied by their lady wives, who then joined Her Majesty The Queen and H.R.H. the Duke of Edinburgh on board the yacht for the opening ceremony. It was not possible for them to stay with us for the whole journey along the Seaway as it was to take us a thousand miles inland to the far reaches of Canada and the United States. Needless to say, there was an obvious amount of American ships and a formidable amount of American forces to be seen, along with ships from different nations.

After the preliminaries of setting sail, we approached our first lock and felt immediately awed by its size. It was almost like entering a giant cave, we were secured with wires and the lock gates were closed and we rose on the incoming water at what seemed like lift speed. On reaching the top level it was necessary to 'scandalise' the top of the mast down to have clearance under the iron structures over the lock. The seaway had now been officially opened!

We were to repeat this operation 31 times during the cruise! For now the first hurdle had been completed successfully. The St. Lambert's Lock was succeeded by the St. Catherine's Lock, the Victoria Bridge by the Power Cables, the Honore Mercier, and the C. P. R. bridges. The yachtsmen locked and unlocked 'scandalised', and rehoisted as the hot day went by. The crowds waved and cheered and boats buzzed about us. 'Britannia' slid on through the Seaway; a famous ship on one of her greatest days. At five o'clock in the afternoon we reached the lower Beauharnois Lock, where the President, Prime Minister and their wives left us, borne away by shining helicopters from the lock side.

The day had gone so well that H.M. The Queen was pleased and 'instructed' the Admiral to 'splice the mainbrace' the next day. This was the order for a double ration of rum for the whole crew! A very welcome gesture, appreciated by one and all. It turned out that we would need a little fortitude for the second day of the inauguration as it was to turn out to be a very trying time.

The second day of the proceedings was shattered by the arrival of heavy fog. The yacht did its best to feel its way along the Seaway, but had to go to anchor twice because it was impossible to see anything. It must be remembered H.M. The Queen was aboard and great care needed to be taken. All this made us five hours late at Snell Lock where the Queen and Prince Philip were due to leave for an appointment with Vice President Nixon, for the opening of the Moses-Saunders Power Dam. They rejoined the yacht at the Iroquois Lock that evening where we had moved onto while they were away. In the procedure at that lock, while rising on the incoming water, we came level with the top of the lock and therefore came eye to eye with the gathered crowds. One gent shouted to the Marine Sergeant Arnold 'Hey Limey, what do you think of Canada?'. To which Ted answered 'Yeah, it's not bad for a colony'.

The third day 29th June saw us on the way to Toronto. It turned out to be a very hot trip indeed,

The Prime Minister of Canada Mr. Diefenbaker, H.R.H. The Duke of Edinburgh, Mrs. Diefenbaker, H.M. The Queen, President of The U.S.A. and Mrs. Eisenhower

way up in the nineties but that was acceptable for we were now in Lake Ontario, and free of locks for some time. We were escorted all the way by three U.S. Coastguard boats on one side and three Canadian police boats on the other, who had their work cut out trying to control the masses of small craft buzzing around us. I could understand their excitement though, for this was a momentous occasion for them. A spectacle that they would never see again.

The first lock St. Lambert, day one

Our arrival at Toronto was well received, and they had built a three tier stand on the dockside to enable many people to view the yacht, and possibly see the Queen and the Prince, on their goings and arrivals for we were due to stay here until July 1st.

During our short stay offers by the population to take some of the crew into their homes to give us a welcome break, were received, and readily accepted. Myself and two of my 'oppos' were accommodated by a young family, who were extremely kind and took us on trips to places of interest.

One of these trips was to the Niagara Falls. A truly wonderful sight, we did the whole thing, even to the tunnels that took us to a viewing platform behind the Falls.

After our two day break, it was back to business. We began the first day of July by leaving Toronto, for a journey through the lock of the Wellar Canal that transported us from Lake Ontario into Lake Erie. I was of the opinion that this journey had been very well planned, for this was Dominion Day for Canada, and the crowds on the lock sides were enormous, waving and cheering, and very excited. So much so that quite a lot of the older generation were moved to tears. Reflecting on those days, I wished the people who consequently were responsible for removing the Royal Yacht from service could have been there to witness that day for I am sure that their decisions would have been influenced to a more favourable outcome for 'Britannia'.

Our journey continued across Lake Erie, and the following morning entered the Detroit River passing the giant Ford Industries and onto our berth at Windsor, which lies directly opposite the city of Detroit. We were only due to stay here for one day, but others like myself were determined to visit this famous American landmark. This we did by being transported by bus through the tunnel under the river. The tunnel, very much like Blackwall, was divided halfway with a thick black line with the American flag down one side, and the Canadian flag on the other, both with the words 'Welcome to'.

The visit was good, and we were treated with a great deal of kindness and curiosity by the Americans. For most of us, it was our first encounter with the sight of skyscrapers, and left us in a state of shock at the sight of such huge structures. The Royal Party were due to rejoin us at Windsor after travelling by train on a tour of Ontario. While awaiting their arrival the Royal Marine Band entertained the tremendous crowds that had gathered in the park next to our berth which seemed to turn into an open air dance. Everyone enjoyed themselves. The great moment came when H.M. The Queen and Prince Philip returned on board to continue our progress to Sarnia for fuel, and then on to Chicago.

Our stay at Sarnia was brief and incidentally my 28th birthday; the 3rd July. We moved onto Georgian Bay where the Royal Party was due to leave us for another train journey tour. The yacht was still surrounded by lots of boats while at anchor in the bay, and we were treated to the odd sight of a seaplane landing and being manoeuvred through the throngs of boats taking up a position not far away from us. The pilot, who seemed to be quite an old chap jumped out onto the floats of his plane and started to eat his sandwiches! When he finished those he calmly climbed back in and flew off. It just shows you how the other half live.

Our stay was brief at Georgian Bay, and we moved off to Parry Sound some distance away across Lake Huron. We arrived there at dusk, to receive H.M. The Queen, Prince Philip, accompanied by P.M. Diefenbaker and Mrs Diefenbaker for our triumphal progress into Chicago.

All this time during the coming's and going's of our trip, my boat driving period had been going from bad to worse for on one occasion I had forgotten to remove the friction locks on the throttles, thus making me shoot straight past the returning liberty men waiting on the jetty before I had realized what was happening. Then there was an incident when a tug was called to pull the yacht off the jetty, to allow my escort boat to be lowered into the resulting gap and I was to shoot the boat out through the alley provided before the tide forced the yacht back onto the harbour wall. The only trouble was that I was a little slow, which resulted in much screaming and hollering from the deck above us to 'Get a bloody move on!' which spurred me on so that we made it with just inches to spare.

One unfortunate incident occurred when I was supposed to rise early with my boat's crew to take the jollyboat to the buoy we were moored to. This enabled the seamens' working party to replace the anchor cable with a wire hawser so that the yacht could slip the moorings easily. Quite an important job, the only trouble was that I didn't get up when called, and went back to sleep. Fortunately Petty Officer Tom Brydon was at hand and he did the job for me, but he was not a happy bunny, and let me have it with both barrels.

To cut a long story short, I spoke to C.P.O. Micky Hunter that I suspected that Lt. South didn't like me very much, and could I request a job change. He returned in about fifteen minutes and informed me that I was perfectly correct, Lt. South didn't like me and that I was to be given back my old job in the laundry, yippee! The boat party was sorry to see me go, ha ha, but it was all for the best as they were never sure what I would do next.

Our arrival into Chicago was both exciting and noisy, as we had grown to expect on this trip. But if Detroit took us by surprise, then Chicago really shook us. There seemed to be a ten lane highway running along the coastline, and the skyscraper laden city beyond that was sheer magic. The novel idea, to us, of having the railway above the street level was really out of the ordinary. We had also marvelled at the Mackinack bridge that we had passed under, for we were unable to see the other end. Once again our stay was for two days but this afforded me the chance to go ashore, and at one point stand at the bottom of the Chicago Tribune building, and on looking up it appeared to be leaning over. The people were very good, and we manage to sample a good deal of their beer, that of course goes without saying.

148

Our arrival in Chicago

The Americans welcomed the Queen's and the Prince's visit, and they seemed to love them both, which always struck me as rather strange, when you consider past history. The British managed to secure America by wresting it from the French, then went on to do the same in Canada. When the War of Independence took place the Americans beat the British only with great help from the French. When that was won they asked the German monarch to be head of their country. Fortunately this request was turned down, otherwise the language would probably be German now and we also would not have been doing the honours of opening the Seaway.

The actual arrival into Chicago was phenomenal, with the American bombers and fighter aircraft flying over the bay with a thunderous noise; and giant coloured water fountains shooting into the air both in the harbour and on the land, all of which made the whole scene somewhat spectacular. It was reliably reported that there were two million people lining the streets in hope of seeing the Royal Party, President Eisenhower, and Mr Diefenbaker pass by in the parade.

All this was taking place at a point two thousand miles from the nearest sea port, and 140 feet above sea level. Also it was the first time since 1813 that the Royal Navy had ventured this far. Bearing all these facts in mind one could not help but feel that history was being made here and feel proud of taking part in it.

Following the norm for this trip our stay was not to be a long one, and we were soon off the following day into Lake Superior heading for the final destination of our journey, Sault-Ste-Marie, and Port Arthur.

These places were as far as we could go into the Seaway, it was also the place that H.M. The Queen and the Duke were due to leave us to continue their tour of Canada, we would not see them again for three weeks until Montreal where they were due to preside over official dinners and functions.

During this time we would make our way back along the Seaway and this turned out to be every bit as exciting as the inward journey. The only difference was that instead of going into the giant locks and being squashed up against the lock wall by the pressure of the water when the lock was flooded, we were now in locks that were having the water let out, and this had a more agreeable effect on the yacht. Now the Royal party were no longer aboard the public were allowed much nearer to us, so at every lock they would gather to get up close. At one of these locks just as we were about to descend and during the banter that was taking place between those crew on the deck and the public a frail old lady was heard in a loud clear voice shout; 'God bless all and every one of you'. That, my friends, would bring a tear to almost anyone's eyes and showed the esteem that Canadians held for the English.

Between the 18th and 24th July, we had been alongside the jetty in Montreal. During this time the Royals had completed their official engagements and it was time for us to turn to home by way of Murray Bay and Halifax. Murray Bay held a bad memory for us as we managed to lose one of our anchors when it was used in the bay, one of the cable links broke and it plunged 120 fathoms to the sea bed. Fortunately it was recovered later by the Canadians and shipped back to us in the U.K.

On arrival in Halifax the Royal Party reviewed the ships that had been escorting us during the trip, and then boarded the flight to take them back to the U.K. We on the other hand set sail for our next port of call that was to be Aberdeen in Scotland in preparation to take the Royal Family on its annual holiday in the Western Isles. Halfway across the Atlantic a message was received from Buckingham Palace cancelling the trip as H.M. The Queen was expecting her third child, Prince Andrew in the New Year; that meant our duties were finished for 1959.

West Indies again - but with a difference

Our passage back home to Portsmouth was uneventful and was only interrupted by the necessity to refuel at sea, our early return home would mean that we would have a bonus of four uninterrupted months to spend with our families.

But the downside was that the crew would need to be downsized owing to the long period of inactivity. As I pointed out earlier in the book, only a third of the crew were permanent 'yachties', the rest were drawn from general service where they were due to return to now, and when we returned to royal duties a fresh draft would be selected from the navy. This was the system designed to give as many personnel in the Royal Navy an opportunity to serve on the yacht.

We were now established back in our exclusive berth at Whale Island. The long snaking, floating walkway leading from the shore out to the yacht had to be negotiated when leaving or returning whatever the weather, sometimes it would be a little rough and the walkway would be jumping about somewhat. That was O.K. if you were sober but could be hazardous if you were not. Previously Pat and I had moved back to London to try and establish ourselves before I was due to leave the Navy in eighteen months after completing my twelve and a half years service. We had two rooms upstairs in my Mum's house; kitchen and bedroom. A little crowded as we had Lynn by then, it was almost like looking back to the days when my family were living upstairs in 30 Royston Street. Fortunately things changed after I left the Navy and we were lucky enough to rent a whole house two doors away from Mum's.

I was still in my job in the laundry and loving every moment of it for the routine was fairly leisurely and fulfilling. It was possible to see that you were producing a good service. Not only that but the 10% bonus from the whole of the monies earned by the laundry was shared equally among the crew and was more than welcome. Pat used to make a point that we had grown to depend on it.

During this period my mode of transport between Portsmouth and London was my trusty old motorcycle and sidecar, which would take me home and back again on my weekend leaves. The bike was good, but the sidecar was suffering a bit of rot in its plywood floor, so this did not enhance the passengers prospect of staying in one piece I decided that something drastic had to be done.

My game plan was that I was going to bring the sidecar on board to fit it with a new bottom! I had chosen the time as the crew had been downsized to ninety permanent, it was also annual leave time which meant only half of those left would be on two weeks leave, also non-duty men would be ashore, all of which brought the total crew actually on board to about 25 or 30. I had checked with the chief shipwright to get his permission to use the carpenter's workshop, and I had purchased a sheet of marine plywood from the dockyard for a hundred cigarettes. I had also received permission from the duty officer to carry out my scheme, so we were all set!

By now I had been joined by my long time 'oppo' Bert Cousins who was as eager as I was to restore the sidecar to good health. Between us we organised the jollyboat to be lowered into the water, took it to the jetty, loaded the sidecar into it and drove it back to the boat's falls where it was hoisted up sidecar and all. This was deftly handled on board by laughing helpers, and duly installed into the 'chippies' workshop. It was decided to do it this way because we could only imagine the consequences if Bert and I had tried to carry it along our floating walkway from the jetty back to the yacht.

Bert and I pressed on with the job in hand, removing the rotten bottom and using this as a template for the new one. During our off duty hours we would saw, seal, tack and generally do a first class repair job including renewing the interior lining, plus one little feature of installing a secret pocket large enough to hold 100 duty free cigarettes for extra smokes that would not be found by the dockyard police in the event of a random search, nothing more sinister than that. In those days that was the most naughty thing you could do!

The only time that I did anything unfitting for a Royal Yachtsman was when another 'oppo' and I, when on a visit to South Africa were sold at quite a cheap price three or four diamonds! On return to England we took them to a jewellers just outside Liverpool Street Station, who examined them and laughingly said 'Sorry lads but they are only Quartz, but if you do get any of the good stuff don't forget to bring them to me', ah well! There is one born every minute.

Continuing our toils in the workshop, Bert and I were surprised one night when the officer of the watch doing his 9pm rounds decided to investigate the unusual noise coming from the 'chippies' workshop and on opening the door he was confronted by us two covered in sawdust, and looking quite dishevelled and standing to attention in the presence of the inspecting officer. I don't think he was aware of the situation as he looked at both of us in turn, then at the sidecar upside down on the trestles, slowly shook his head in disbelief, quietly closed the door and continued on his rounds without saying a word.

Our idyllic life continued over Christmas up to early January when we were due to sail for the

Princess Alice

West Indies for the tour with Princess Alice, the Princess Royal. The trip across the Atlantic was horrendous some of the worst weather I had ever experienced. Gigantic waves that we were informed measured 60 feet from the trough to the crest.

Unfortunately the two elderly dressers of the Princess were taking passage with us and they suffered very much with sickness and bruising to their bodies as they were thrown about. It eventually passed and we were very glad to get to the warmer climes of our favourite destination where on the 15th January Princess Alice arrived on board for her goodwill tour.

The tour was to last two months taking in a large selection of islands including Trinidad, Tobago, Grenada, Carriacou, St. Vincent, Barbados, St. Lucia, Dominica, Montserrat, Antigua, St. Kitts, Nevis, Anguilla, Tortola,

The finale of Princess Alice's tour with assembled yacht's crew

Jamaica, Stan Creek, Belize, Grand Cayman and Grand Turk. You can see the itinerary was quite large and it would take a lot of time to get around all of those islands without spending much time at each venue.

Princess Alice inspecting the police in Trinidad

Looking back on that trip I am now convinced that the whole cruise was in order that the ground could be laid in preparation for the marriage of Princess Margaret and Mr Armstrong Jones on the following 3rd May 1960 when their honeymoon would lead us back to - yes you have guessed it - West Indies. You would think that we would get a little bored going to the same place, but we old sailors could put up with the balmy weather, rum and cokes, wonderful beaches and slightly leisurely routines. Oh come on, who could not love the West Indies?

Our first port of call was Trinidad where, as you may remember the disaster in the waterside bar took place, putting a few of our crew into the sick bay, as described earlier in the book. Recriminations don't seem to last long, and everyone was on their best behaviour. We moved on through the islands in an orderly way performing our duties in a very professional manner. We had in fact become good at the job. Early morning starts, decks scrubbed, paintwork washed, brasses polished and everything stowed away ready for the appropriate Royal personage to enjoy the privacy that was to be theirs as from 9am onwards! All this was achieved with no spoken words; all directives by hand signal to make sure that the Royals were not disturbed in any way.

As we only stayed at any one place for a short time allowing the crew just a short break for drinks ashore, swimming parties or a visit to a local industry nothing took place that I can bring to mind. Although in Barbados we visited a sugar factory where one of the by-products is of course rum. It was interesting to see how it was extracted. Afterwards we went to the laboratory and were given a small glass of the product on strict instructions not to drink it but only wet our lips and on doing so found that the liquid was quite capable of turning our lips numb!

The one place that did stand out in my mind was Belize situated next to Mexico, probably because we had never visited this area before. This area is now used intensively as a training ground in jungle fighting for British troops.

At the time of our visit to this place it turned out to be some sort of religious holiday but from the pace of the population you would be led to believe that every day was a holiday. There was only one bar open. Of course I have no idea what it's like now, probably a big tourist attraction full of massive hotels and its originality spoilt forever. I can be thankful that I managed to travel the world when I did and was able to see these places as they were, such as Seychelles in the Indian Ocean when a boat only visited once every three months back in 1956 and at that time the women outnumbered the men by seven to one. I am sure that there must be a lot of places untouched by time, but for how long the pleasure seeking populous find and totally destroy them?

The fact finding tour as I call it came to its conclusion on the 7th April and we returned to Portsmouth in the UK by way of the Azores ready to be spruced up for our next exciting venture, the wedding of Princess Margaret, which I must admit at that time we knew nothing about.

Princess Margaret's Wedding Cruise and my Last Voyage

Our journey back to Portsmouth via the Azores was uneventful compared to the outward journey when we were battered by a fierce storm as I described earlier. We at first returned to our usual berth at Whale Island to enjoy a short stay in perfect peace, but later shifted into the dockyard to start refitting for the big event that was to take place in London on the following month of May. This was the first we had heard of the wedding, and it would be our duty to be at berth at the Tower of London ready to receive the bride and groom and take them on their honeymoon to the West Indies for six weeks.

In the dockyard, things followed the same pattern as in other preparations for important trips; the ship's side was repainted to an immaculate bluebottle enamel, white superstructure overhauled as were the boats and general upper deck equipment. Stores and spares were carefully loaded and stored, once again the beer getting special attention, the empty fresh water tanks were filled to the very brim with the amber nectar in handy 24 can packs, for it was paramount to make sure the lads were well catered for. All this frenzy of activity did not affect me very much as I was still safely ensconced in my job in the laundry, the only difference for us was the extra influx of working clothes that the crew were putting in to be cleaned. I was grateful to be there, and I could not help feeling that I was a permanent fixture now as my service in the Royal Navy was due to expire the following year.

I had anticipated that sometime before, and had moved Pat and baby Lynn to London to live upstairs in my mother's house in Bethnal Green. The yacht going to London was going to be a bonus for me as we were destined to arrive nearly a week before the wedding, there would be ample time to spend with them.

Our arrival in the Capital was quite exciting, it was the second time for me to experience this situation, and although it must have been quite a spectacle for the public, it was at the same time an anti-climax as all eyes were fixed on the wedding arrangements. As expected I was able to spend quite a bit of time at home, my father-in-law had the idea of giving a party for any of the lads on board the yacht who would care to come, which turned out to be six for there were so many things being offered by the City of London in the way of entertainment that they were finding it hard to make choices. The appointed six turned up at his house, 71 Ellesmere Road, Bow and we had a riotous time, lots of drink and eats and well wishes from all and sundry. The party went well on into the night and it was a case of sleeping wherever you could find a space once the revelries were over. That left the problem of getting everybody back to the jetty at the Tower of London in time to catch the boat back on board, for it would not do to be adrift. The situation was resolved when my brother-in-law Eric borrowed his Dad's van and packed us all in for a fast run through the city. Now the drawback to a load of matelots that have been well greased the night before is moans and groans, hangovers and worst of all flatulence there is hardly any need to mention that it quickly got very fetid in there bringing on the feeling of nausea. Fortunately Eric made good time but was only able to get as far as Billingsgate Fish Market which in those days was situated at the Tower, or rather to one side of it, but there was time for us to all pile out and make a shortcut through the market.

Our hurried passage through the fish market was halted when a large group of American tourists caught sight or us. 'Oh my God, they are off the Royal Yacht'. 'Do let us take some pictures' So with little time to spare we duly grouped up for them to take their snaps, for they were obviously here for the occasion and would value the photographs a great deal.

I must explain here that I was carrying a bright yellow plastic bucket that I had purchased the day before on behalf of the laundry, for the purpose of mixing starch for the officers collars and boiled evening shirts processed on the machine that I operated. So picture if you can our little group of sailors posing, with me in the middle with this bucket in my hand and the Americans busy snapping away, their backs to a fish lorry that was being unloaded. When one of the fish porters dressed in his hard flat hat that was used to carry the fish baskets on their heads, leaned right across the Americans and shouted at me 'What's the bucket for, Margaret to poop in?'. There were sharp cries of disbelief from the photographers, and smothered laughter from us, but we did wonder how he could have brought himself to be so crude. But there he was a Cockney fish porter!

The week that we were berthed at the Tower awaiting the big day was interesting to say the least, for the offers of entertainment came flooding in from all over London that seemed to be gripped by the fever of the moment and the offers were readily taken up by an enthusiastic crew. As for myself having my family near at hand, my week was filled with going home in the evening and returning on board by eight o'clock by means of catching the 7.30 liberty boat at the floating pontoon just below the Tower of London.

159

Princess Margaret to Mr. Antony Armstrong Jones

Souvenir of the Wedding May 6th 1960

I arrived one morning at the pontoon just in time to see the police unloading a dead body from their launch. It had been fished out of the Thames further up, not a pleasant sight to greet one first thing in the morning. Also during that week I had been having discussions at home with Pat's uncle Harry who was a director of a plant hire company, hiring earth moving machinery to building contractors. He was in fact offering me a job when I had completed my service in the R.N., in the first instance by driving the machines and finding out first hand their capabilities, and then onto a management position. I was impressed with the offer and I considered it as my future role in life. It transpired later that Harry

160

The newlyweds arrive by barge to start their honeymoon

was a bit of a dubious character and things didn't turn out as expected, but that's another story.

The wedding day finally arrived and we were all spick and span ready for the occasion. When all the formalities had been carried out the newlyweds arrived in the Royal Barge ready to embark to start their honeymoon. As soon as they were settled we slipped our moorings and proceeded on our way to the deafening cheers of the well wishers who seemed to occupy every nook and cranny of the riverside. Nearby ships sirens were blasting away and the Royal couple were in a prominent position for quite a long time giving all the public a grand view and waving to the enthusiastic crowds. We made our way along the Thames and finally arrived at the end of the estuary and turned into the English Channel; we were on our way!

The first night outbound was very calm and friendly, and proved to be for the whole crossing of the Atlantic thank goodness. The officers had a celebratory drink with the couple, and we were surprised to discover that a wedding cake had been given to the ship's company to share. It was actually one of seven that was presented during the run up to the wedding, we were of course very pleased with the gesture even in the knowledge that the portions would not be large considering that there were 250 men. I posted mine off to Pat in an airtight tin.

The following morning the duty laundry crew were surprised when they were suddenly ordered to leave the laundry and were even more surprised when along came members of the Palace staff escorted by a couple of Royal Marines bearing piles of bed sheets which they placed in the large washing machines that we had been instructed to leave open. It was only when the water and washing liquid had been applied, that it dawned on us that these were the first night bedclothes that were being processed! I must admit we all thought it was a bit over the top, but never mind.

The weather gradually improved as the days went by, games were organised for upper deck sports and we all looked forward to the day when we would start hearing the Caribbean radio music, always a good sign that we were getting quite near. The Royal couple were of course given the best privacy that could be managed, so it was an oversight when one of the seamen, Bill Mesher, was sent aft to rig up the safety nets requested that were used when the game of quoits was being played. In doing so Bill inadvertently observed Armstrong Jones taking intimate photographs of the Princess in what state of dress I would hate to take a guess at. It wasn't his fault for the deck he was on overlooked the one below, an objection was forthcoming, and Bill being the nervous character he was could not help but be embarrassed by it all. But it was all sorted out and life returned to being as normal as can be expected. At last the Caribbean music came through loud and clear and we knew that we had arrived.

We arrived at our first destination; which was the first in the designated itinerary of Tobago, Trinidad, Cays, Mustique, Dominica, Antigua and then officially back to Portsmouth all in six weeks. Ho hum, as I have mentioned before someone had to do it!

The stay at Tobago didn't last long before we were off meandering among the islands stopping wherever it took their fancy for we were not on official Royal duty, they were on honeymoon. I know

we were supposed to be unescorted, but I felt sure that the combined Services of Great Britain were keeping an eye on us. One island we stopped at for the Royal Party to land for a picnic and swimming, we the crew were offered the chance to take advantage of the other side of the island to sample the delights of the pure white sands and blue sea for a refreshing dip. The only trouble was, that the launch that took twenty of us there was only able to get within a hundred yards of the beach, as this was very shallow. That meant we had to swim onto the beach. I was very nervous of doing this, for as we were travelling in I spotted two large sharks diving under the boat. When I conveyed this information to the rest of the lads all they said was, rubbish, you must have been seeing things. But being convinced that I was not seeing things I

declined the offer to swim in and stayed on the boat. Fortunately nobody was eaten and all ended well. Incidentally if you were wondering, a small dinghy from their boat to the beach rowed the couple in.

Trinidad was a blast as usual for we had become frequent visitors there, what with the great calypso songs that continually seemed to come from everywhere around us. One of the main artists was a man who called himself the Mighty Sparrow and one of the favourite calypsos was Crazy Love which we heard so many times that I knew the words off by heart and always surprised the native population by singing loudly along with the record or steel band when it was played.

Being read the riot act after the big punch up at one of the bars on a previous visit, it was decided the new venue for the 'yachties' when ashore was to

be the slightly upmarket nightspot The Pepper Pot.

It was a very good choice, for it was frequented by a lot of the non-native population, thus avoiding any unwanted provocation. The visit was a success, the couple received a big reception from all to congratulate them, and before long we were on our way to the next venue; Mustique.

This is a place that was also very familiar to us owing to our past visit during the sadder days for H.R.H. when she was not given permission by H.M. The Queen to marry Group Captain Townsend. But things had taken a turn for the better now and the couple were to be given the best reception ever by Colin Tennant who owned the island, and was a very good friend of Princess Margaret. They were not only going to have the privacy of the yacht but even more privacy when ashore, having their own beach and house.

There were other residents living on Mustique but they had been carefully chosen by Colin Tennant who had the right to determine who did, or did not reside. All in all they had a wonderful time there, and I am sure they were sad to leave when the time came to continue the cruise. It seems strange when looking back to those happy times how drastically the situation changed in later years. Things went wrong between Margaret and Lord Snowdon to a point where they divorced and Margaret spent a lot of time back in Mustique in her house in company of a young man called Roddy Llewellyn. She apparently smoked too much and eventually died of what seemed to be lung cancer. Such a sad end.

After a further visit to Dominica and Antigua the Royal couple left us to fly home to the U.K. The whole trip had been a great success for all concerned and one of the last memorable experiences for me. The yacht once again turned for home and our next duty of Cowes Week at the Isle of Wight.

As predicted we started our cruise on the 30th July at Cowes Week and then continued onto the Western Isles trip taking in Lerwick, Fetlar, Baltasound, Uyeasound, Mid Yell, Whalsay, Fair Isle, Stromness, Kirkwall, Stronsay, Westray and finally back to Aberdeen where the family would disembark and take up residence at Balmoral Castle. Looking at the list of ports of call you could almost imagine you were visiting another country, couldn't you?

The Western Isles trips were always very pleasant as far as we were concerned for it was always slightly informal even though the whole Royal Family were aboard, this time they included; H.M. The Queen, H.R.H. Prince Philip, Ann and Charles, Princess Alexandra and Prince Michael of Kent. So you can see that we had quite a large gathering of Royals to tend to. They liked to have free and easy days, for this was their annual holiday. Boats for fishing and exploring would be made ready at a moment's notice whenever they decided on a plan. H.M. The Queen was a very keen follower of the unexpected in this respect and could be seen enthusiastically organising the day's events. On one fishing trip though disaster struck when Prince Charles in his excitement fell over the side of the moving boat. One of the boat's crew immediately dived into the cold waters and rescued Charles by holding him up until the boat could be turned around to get him back on board. I am given to understand that H.M. The Queen suitably rewarded young A.B. Seaman Apps, the rescuer.

At the end of the trip the Royal Family disembarked at Aberdeen. There was a coach trip for any of the interested crew through Deeside and a visit to Balmoral. Finally a visit to Crathie Church, which of course is the preferred church used by the Royal family when at Balmoral. Britannia then turned her bow towards the south and home to Portsmouth.

This for me was the last journey I was to make on the yacht for I discovered that no more trips were planned until April the following year, it was a mixture of sadness, apprehension, and maybe a little excitement. Was I doing the right thing by not signing on for a further five years service which I would most certainly serve on the yacht? Or was I right to go back into civvy street and take my chances in a very commercial world? The discussion still continues now between Pat and myself seeing that some of my fellow 'yachties' did sign on and spent thirty years on board and in Royal Service all that time, even moving into other Royal employment at Buckingham Palace and Windsor Castle when their time in the Navy was over.

Still I did make the choice to go. After a period at Portsmouth and a couple of interviews with my divisional officer as to whether I had made the right decision I was drafted off the yacht and into H.M.S. Sultan for a month's course on welding. I had chosen this as I was of the opinion that it would probably help in my new employment. It did actually help but not right away. I enjoyed my four weeks course at Sultan and the circumstances were a bit strange for it was backing onto the naval housing estate that Pat and I had moved out of some time ago after spending a few very happy years living there among good friends and neighbours. Even more strange was the fact that I went back there again quite a few years later to take part in a senior soldiers course to comply with my training with the Army to become a sergeant instructor in the Army cadet force, Royal Green Jackets.

On the completion of my welding course they moved me over to the naval barracks at Portsmouth for my final release and a bounty of one hundred and thirty pounds which seemed like a lot of money then. I spent a miserable month there doing aimless jobs like looking after barrack sweeping parties whose only ambition seemed to be to skive off the moment you did not watch them. I even had a short spell in the mail sorting room.

Finally on the 2nd July 1961 I was given new civilian clothing and my bounty. I had fulfilled my boyhood dreams and sailed a total of 164,252 nautical miles on the Royal Yacht and still remain in the family of 'yachties' through our association to this very day.

Lament for Britannia

I have watched her leave port for a distant shore,
as she flew the flag for a Royal Tour.
A part of Old England wherever she goes,
And for who she earned millions, (not everyone knows)
O.K. she's fifty but she still looks great,
And the powers that be who decided her fate,
Should have watched as she sailed to her port of call,
Or have seen her at anchor dressed 'overall'.
A replacement could never, no way be the same,
Ask all who've served on her and are proud of her name.
To hundreds of sailors she was 'home' through the years,
When decommissioned I know there were tears,
Especially ex-yachties who knew her so well,
Their feelings and memories forever they'll tell.
So Rule the Waves Britannia, the order must be,
For her like again we never shall see.

Mrs. P. Saxby